Side Man

SIDE MAN

by
Warren Leight

STAGE
&SCREEN
The Book Club for the Performing Arts

Garden City, New York

ISBN 0-7394-0072-X
PRINTED IN THE UNITED STATES OF AMERICA

Author's Note

I avoided writing *Side Man* for twenty years. This was probably for the best, because during my years as a writer-for-hire, I gained a little perspective and shed a little anger.

After all the rehearsals and performances, I've learned a few things about the playing of the play. Gene, the father, exists in sort of a bubble. When the conversation isn't about music, he's elsewhere; even if he's talking to you. Actors who are used to engaging will find this frustrating. Actors who play Clifford will also be frustrated because he too is a bit of a side man. If anyone asks, Clifford is always "fine." He does not want to show us everything he is feeling, nor is he even aware of it for most of the play. He feels the same responsibility to the audience that he did to his parents—he keeps things up as much as possible, for as long as he can.

If the side men keep their emotions in check, Terry, the mother, kind of airs hers out. But the actress playing her should not embrace her craziness. Instead, fight for Terry and for her side of the story. Also, no matter how angry she gets, Terry cares deeply for her husband and especially her son.

The other side men, and Patsy also come with a lot of mileage. I think of Jonesy as looking out for Terry; Patsy as Clifford's guardian; and Al and Ziggy as Gene's section-mates. On stage at least, they cover him. Even though no one actually manages to stop the family's slide, they all do as much as they can. As did all the real life side men and family members on whom these characters are based.

Finally, if you get the chance, listen to the music of this world; to the trumpet kings: Clifford Brown, Fats Navarro, Red Rodney, Lee Morgan, Dizzy, Miles, Chet; and to the side men who played, night after night, with Claude Thornhill, Charlie Barnett, Buddy Rich and Woody Herman.

Special Thanks

When I finally began to write *Side Man* I received generous, unconditional support and insight from a number of actors, directors, musicians, writers, designers, stage crew and producers. I also received guidance and love from dozens of friends and strangers who have gone through personal dramas like the family in this play. It's been humbling.

I am completely indebted to Michael Mayer for his long devotion to *Side Man*. For his gentle guidance ("this scene is heinous"). For his feel for this world, and for how to make it come to life on stage. Of course, he and I were lucky. We've had good homes: the West Bank, Powerhouse, CSC, and the Roundabout. In addition to the generous actors and designers listed on the following pages, I was helped by: Jeff Binder, Patrick Breen, Nicole Burdette, Geoffrey Cantor, Suzanne Dottino, Tim Guinee, David Henderson, Don Holder, Felicity Huffman, Brian Keane, Bill Lang, Marissa Matrone, Dan Moran, Geoffrey Nauffts, Jack O'Connor, Austin Pendleton, Neil Pepe, and Roger Raines.

Thanks also to a number of the show's Guardian Angels: Peter Manning, who knowingly guided the play on its long journey from Poughkeepsie to Broadway; Jay Harris and the Weissberger Group, who stepped forward early and often. More thanks to: Robbie Baitz, Len Berkmann, Andre Bishop, Eric Bogosian, Jo Bonney, Susann

Brinkley, Anne Brooks, Jim Carnahan, Susan Chicoine, Stephanie Coen, Lee Cohen, Burt Collins, Erin Dunn, Beth Emelson, Peter Flaxman, Jenny Gersten, William Goldman, Todd Haimes, Holly Harper, Beth Henley, Ron Kastner, Rob Kaufelt, William Kennedy, Mimi Kramer, George Lane, Nile Lanning, Don, Edward, Jody, and Timmy Leight, Local 802, Evan Lurie, Mary Meagher, Peter Marks, Max Mayer, John McCormack, NYSF, Johnny Olson, Daryl Roth, Rudd Simmons, Gary Springer, and Ron Taft.

Side Man Chronology

Side Man was written while Warren was a member of the New York Playwright's Lab. It was work-shopped by Naked Angels in the basement of the West Bank Cafe (February 1996), and was originally produced in June 1996 by New York Stage and Film at Vassar's Powerhouse Theatre.

After its New York City premiere, *Side Man* was nominated for the John Gassner Playwriting Award, and several Outer Circle and Drama Desk Awards, including Best Play. Warren won Newsday's Oppenheimer Award given to the Best New American Playwright, and the George and Elisabeth Marton Playwriting Award in the fall of 1998.

Warren Leight's *Side Man* was first produced in New York City on March 11, 1998. It was produced by The Weissberger Theater Group (Jay Harris, Producer) and Peter Manning. It was directed by Michael Mayer. The set designs were by Neil Patel, the costume designs were by Tom Broecker, hair and wigs by Bobby H. Grayson, the lighting design was by Kenneth Posner and the sound design was by Raymond D. Schilke. The production stage manager was Andrea J. Testani.

THE CAST
(In order of appearance)

Clifford...........Robert Sella
Terry...........Edie Falco
Patsy.............Angelica Torn
Gene..............Frank Wood
Al.................Joseph Lyle Taylor
Ziggy............Michael Mastro
Jonesy............Kevin Geer

Side Man premiered on Broadway as the first new play to be produced at the Roundabout Theatre Company's Main Stage on June 25th, 1998. Todd Haimes was artistic director and Jay Adler was production supervisor. Wendy Makkena replaced Edie Falco in the role of Terry.

On November 8th, 1998, *Side Man* re-opened at the John Golden Theatre with new co-producers Ron Kastner, James Cushing, and Joan Stein and general manager Roy Gabay. Christian Slater replaced Robert Sella in the role of Clifford.

For side men,
and their families

ACT ONE

ACT I

Downstage center, lights up on the slightly awkward, twenty-nine-year-old Clifford. To his right, an old bar. Downstage left, a circular booth and table. Clifford faces the audience.

Clifford: It's almost . . . *(looks at watch)* oh, I'm late. I'm sure it has nothing to do with the fact that I'm seeing my parents tonight.

Both of them: Mom *and* Dad, a kind of *This Is Your Life* bender.

I'm not seeing them together, mind you. *Not* a good idea. Definitely not a good idea. Once, long ago, this trumpet player, who I'll probably also see tonight, told me: "The rocksh in her head fit the wholesh in hish."

Not anymore. They haven't seen each other, and I haven't seen him in—

So, OK, it's complicated.

Plus, if I see past all the . . . history, I sense, and this one really screws me up, that things would have been better for them if they'd never had me. But,

they did. I'm on the scene, as my old man would
say. And even though there are no clean breaks, I
swear, tomorrow morning I'm out. So tonight, before the "big reunion" with my father, I have a
farewell dinner at Mom's, in the zip code of my
youth . . .

(*Lights up on Clifford's mom, Terry. She stands in the
doorway to her off-stage bedroom, smoking a cigarette,
alone*)

Terry: Don't start with me, Clifford—I'm not going
over there.

Clifford: Ma—I wasn't asking you to—

Terry: I can't stand to hear him play—

Clifford: I just wanted you to know I was—

Terry: I already knew. I had a dream you saw him.
And you know what pissed me off? He hasn't aged.
He'll never age—nothing gets to him—

Clifford: Well, I—

Terry: Don't stick up for him Clifford. You know
he gaslit me. Everyone thinks your father's so
sweet: "Poor Gene, clean Gene, sweet Gene. How
he suffers with crazy Terry."

Clifford: No one says—

Terry: That rat-bastard *gaslit* me. (*Quick shift, concerned now*) How does he look? *Is he eating?*

Clifford: What?

Terry: Your father. In the dream. He looked thin.

Clifford: How should I know? I haven't seen him.

Terry: I made lasagne; there's some containers in the freezer. He can't even feed himself. Will you be home for Christmas?

Clifford: I don't know.

Terry: You better get going, have a good time . . . there's a box in the hallway with some old photos and magazines. I thought you could use them for your art projects.

Clifford: Thanks, Ma.

Terry: And tomorrow, on the plane—

Clifford: I know Ma: "Say hello to the pilot" when I board.

Terry: It keeps them alert, if they meet the passengers. Responsible.

Clifford: I know, Ma.

(*She snuffs out her cigarette, as the lights go out on her. Clifford now walks in The Melody Lounge. From an un-*

seen bandstand, a trumpet player solos on I Remember Clifford)

Clifford: I walk in and I hear him before I see him. Playing a ballad. You could play me a hundred trumpet solos and I'd know which one was his. My father's voice. (*Listens a bit, fights getting over-whelmed by the music. Goes over to a seat at the bar. Clifford takes it in*)

When I was a kid, I thought The Melody Lounge was the coolest place on Earth. In high school, where I was a complete loser, the only thing I had going for me was bringing the guys here to see my old man play trumpet. I was drinking screwdrivers at this bar from the time I was thirteen.

They sound good tonight. All of them. Up there, on the bandstand, a little over two hundred years of musical experience. Ziggy and my dad and Al and Jonesy keep time so well that it's kind of stood still for them, at least when they're playing. They were all horn players in the legendary, completely forgotten Claude Thornhill big band. They re-corded things on *wire* in the forties, right after the war, that are still too hip for the room. (*Looks around*) Not that there's anyone in the room tonight. In the audience there's me, two drunks from Jersey, and (*turns to see*) . . . Patsy?

(*Patsy has walked past the bar and now sees Clifford. She is in her late fifties, but you'd never know it. In her heyday, she stopped traffic on 52nd Street. She hugs him as they speak*)

Patsy: Clifford? Is that you? I haven't seen you in . . . forever. Does your father know you're here?

Clifford: It's kind of a surprise.

Patsy (*looks him over*)**:** You haven't changed—

Clifford: Don't tell my shrink—she'd be heartbroken.

Patsy: No, you haven't—when you were six, you looked thirty, and you still look thirty . . . So, how's work?

Clifford: I quit.

Patsy: Good for you.

Clifford: I'm going west.

Patsy: You *have* changed.

Clifford (*changing the subject*)**:** *You* haven't. You look great.

Patsy: What can I say, it's my cross to bear. . . . How's Terry?

Clifford: I just came from there—

(*Lights up on Terry. Music out. She stands in the doorway to her off-stage bedroom, smoking a cigarette, alone*)

Terry: Clifford, what's the name of that Tiny Kahn tune?

Clifford *(to audience)*: She does this to me all the time, even when she's not here, she's here. *(To Terry) Just My Fucking Luck?*

Terry: No, not Kahn, the other one—

Clifford: Kern? *Why Was I Born?*

Terry *(she nods)*: Yes.

Clifford *(turns to the audience)*: You kind of have to work with her.

Terry: Ask your father to play it.

(She closes door, as lights go out on her. Music up again: I Remember Clifford)

Clifford: OK Ma, *Why Was I Born?* I'll ask.

Patsy: Yoo hoo, Clifford.

Clifford *(he returns to Patsy)*: Sorry.

Patsy: How is she?

Clifford: Terry? Good days . . . bad days.

(She doesn't push him)

Patsy: Old days. You know, (*looks across the stage to the empty booth*) they had their first date here.

Clifford: Their only date, I think.

Patsy: Once upon a time Clifford, we were in our prime . . . (*she hugs him*) It's been too long.

Clifford (*to audience, during the hug*): Years, actually. Time flies when it crawls. (*To Patsy*) These guys together . . . I can't even think of the last time that happened.

(*Terry re-opens her door. Music out. Patsy retreats up-stage*)

Terry: Well, you know it wasn't on a family vacation or at a restaurant. Or a party. *Your* father never took us anywhere.

Clifford: Ma, please—

Terry: All of them—if they're not on a club date, their idea of a big get-together is when they sign for their unemployment check.

(*Terry closes her door*)

Clifford (*to audience*): She can be a little . . . dark. But she's usually right. The last time I saw these guys together *was* at Unemployment. Nine years ago, at the old 92nd Street Office. The musicians called it Club 92.

(Harsh lights up on Club 92. Clifford stands, walks over to the head of the beginner's unemployment line. Two lines away, his father, Gene, and Al, Ziggy, and Jonesy wait on the old-timer's line)

Clifford *(to audience)*: I am twenty-one years old, out of college, out of work. On line for my first unemployment check. It is 1977. As I inch my way up the beginner's line, I spot my father, who is over there *(points)* to sign for what, his four millionth check. As a jazz musician, he is sort of always there. There's the National Endowment for the Arts, which is money for classical musicians, and there's the New York State Bureau of Unemployment, which gives grants to jazz musicians. It's a two-tiered system.

(Gene calling out to the other musicians)

Gene: Al, Ziggy, Jonesy—get a load of this: My kid is signing for his first check.

(The guys all see Clifford, shout hellos and wave)

Clifford: He is, at that moment, prouder of me than I have ever seen him: Today, I am a man. *(Clifford joins Gene, Al, Ziggy and Jonesy in a booth at the Melody Lounge)*

Clifford *(to audience)*: To celebrate, the old man takes me out afterwards. The guys are in a booth at the back. You can always spot them: they wear car coats, caps, *a lot of* brown and tan polyester; and they sit as far away from daylight as possible.

Gene *(pointing to Clifford)*: *My son my son. (To the guys)* Did you see him?

(Handshakes of congratulation)

Al: Mazel tov.

Ziggy: Gesundheit.

Al: Thank you.

(Clifford, beaming, now turns back to the audience)

Clifford: It's a special day. And it will prove to be the only time in my life I'll see my father pick up a check: Not that Al, Ziggy, or Jonesy picks up a check either. Musicians don't pick up checks. They don't dance. They don't buy when they can rent. They don't care about clothes, shoes, or light. Or weather, except in terms of how it might effect alternate-side of the street parking. They order soup:

(The waitress comes. It's Patsy. Eight years younger)

Al: I'll have the . . . soup.

Ziggy: Ish there a shpecial shoup?

Jonesy: What do you care? Four soups, Patsy.

(Patsy exits to get soups)

Jonesy: You want one kid? Five—make it five. Or four soups, one shoup, for Ziggy.

Ziggy: Shcrew you. Schmuck. (*Shouting*) And um, extra crackersh.

(*Patsy brings the soups and crackers.*)

Clifford (*to audience*): Soups come. They wait ten minutes for them to cool down; they're horn players, they can't burn their chops. After a while, I become aware that Jonesy, who has one eye and used to play trombone, is staring at me. Or my arms.

(*Jonesy stares at Clifford's rolled-up shirt sleeves, or more accurately, at the veins in his exposed forearms*)

Jonesy: Gene, your kid has great rope. Man—

Clifford (*to audience*): What do you say when an ex-junkie compliments your veins? (*To Jonesy*) Thank you.

Jonesy (*to Gene, very sweet*): No, he does. I wouldn't have said it if I didn't mean it. I mean, Christ, by the time I was his age, I'd shot out so many veins I was reduced to shooting between my toes.

Ziggy: We're eating. Ish it too much to ashk . . .

Jonesy: Or maybe at that time I was still between my fingers.

Ziggy: Thank you. That'sh better.

Jonesy: Lost my eye in the war.

(He pops his glass eye out and shows it to Clifford and the guys)

Ziggy: He shpent the war teaching retarded buglersh reveille.

Jonesy: The home front was very dangerous.

Al: Ask Dicky Smith.

(Everyone laughs. Al explains the reference to Clifford)

Al: Piano player, poor schmuck, gets his notice. Now Dickie was clean at that time.

Ziggy: A Mormon.

Clifford *(to the audience)***:** A Mormon: this means, a little pot, a couple of times a day. Benzedrine inhalers. Booze.

Al: *Clean.* But he's pissing in his pants about being called up. There was a very big war going on at the time.

Ziggy: Enormoush.

Al: And little Dickie—he doesn't want any part of it. So he goes to Jonesy and says, fix me up. (*Explaining to Clifford*) He figures, if he's a junkie, he's automatic 4-F.

Clifford: Got it—

Jonesy: I tried to warn him—kid, I said, it's so good, don't even try it once. (*To Clifford*) Which is actually what someone said to me when I first started. Which of course only made me want to try it all the more. (*For the table*) So I show him the ropes. What I didn't know, is he's also got someone lobbing him bennies—

Ziggy and Al (*singing*): *Everytime it rains it rains, bennies from heaven.*

Jonesy: And he's knocking back about a quart of bourbon a day. Beer chasers. He spends three weeks just about killing himself, *then* they postpone his friggin' physical. Now by this point, he's pretty strung out—

Al: He can't stop even if he wants to—

Jonesy: Which you never do, by the way.

Ziggy: —Sho he'sh mainlining and taking uppersh and drinking and he'sh loshing weight caushe he'sh vomiting sho much.

Al: And he's got the shakes. And he hasn't slept in weeks. And finally—

Jonesy: They call him in—and he can barely drag his ass up the stairs. He's down to about ninety-five pounds, his eyes are like bulging out of his forehead. He's lost his hair. He's a total friggin' mess—they take one look at him—they say: "Pal, no point in even giving you a physical"—get this:

Jonesy, Ziggy, Al: "You're too fuckin' short."

(The guys laugh ahead of the punchline, and through it)

Clifford *(to audience)*: The musicians love this story.

Ziggy: Too short.

(The guys break up again)

Ziggy: You get it? He wash like five-two. None of ush ever thought about it. Piano. What differensh did it make?

Jonesy: They never even noticed he was a junkie. Me though, I wasn't a junkie then so much as an addict—

Al: Ah-huh.

Clifford *(to audience)*: It's a subtle distinction.

Jonesy: But these southern bases were so friggin' hot you had to wear short sleeves all the time, so I can't shoot into my arms, so I'm between my fingers, my toes, and then, into my eye—

Ziggy: I would argue thish makesh him a junkie, but—

Jonesy: *So* I had to shoot into my *eye*. Which only worked for a while.

Al: And that's how he got the Purple Heart—

Jonesy: —and *lifetime* partial disability.

(The guys all salaam-bow to him)

Ziggy *(to Clifford)*: Even though he'sh already got dishability, he shtill comesh down every week to shign for hish unemployment check. *(Half-serious)* That'sh a work ethic.

Jonesy: *Thank you.* I told the sergeant if I had to go home to Ohio—

Clifford *(to audience)*: He was from the Bronx—they all were.

Jonesy: —with a jaundiced, pus-leaching sore where my eye—

Ziggy: Jesush Chrisht. Can anyone eat with thish?

(Al and Jonesy raise their hands)

Gene: The eyes have it.

(Everyone laughs. Dad winks at Clifford)

Clifford *(to audience)*: These are my role models. My authority figures. My—

Jonesy *(to Clifford)*: Hey kid. What kind of horn do you play?

Gene *(to Jonesy)*: Bite your tongue. *(To Clifford)* Someone has to make a living in the family.

Ziggy: I remember when you wanted leshons. Your old lady shaid no shon of hersh would ever do to another woman what he *(points to Gene)* did to her.

Al and Ziggy *(imitating the mother)*: "The rat-bastard."

(Everyone laughs at this)

Gene: He's still my boy. Managed to get twenty weeks on the books—as a painter.

Al: Houses?

Clifford: Collages. School job. I cut and paste these—

Gene: The kid got a scholarship to some painting school.

Clifford *(to audience)*: RISD. Grad school . . .

Gene: But instead, he's gonna write for TV. *(To Clifford)* Right?

Ziggy *(impressed)*: TV? That'sh a pretty good field. Your father and I were going to do that once.

Clifford: I know, I know. But it's not TV—it's advertising. Maybe. I'm up for something.

Ziggy: TV paysh pretty good.

Clifford: If I get it, yeah. Like twelve hundred a week. But it's not—*(To audience)* The money stops the group cold.

Gene: You cop that kind of bread—you work three weeks, you can lay out the whole year.

(Everyone agrees)

Clifford *(to audience)***:** You're listening to jazzonomics. The theory that—

Gene: You keep your nut small, you pay your dues, you get to blow your horn.

Al: Wait, wait, wait . . . Twelve hundred a week? You mean a month, right?

Gene: As long as you got a place to flop, the rest is . . . *(He spaces out)*

Clifford *(to audience)***:** There is no rest. From the time I was four, I knew the family was headed for financial ruin.

Jonesy: You gonna finish your crackers?

(Jonesy pockets a few cracker packets)

Clifford: From the time I was six, I, and everyone else knew, it would be up to me to save us.

Gene: I heard about people making money with money, but I always figured that was a sick head to get into—

Clifford *(to audience)*: Jazzonomics is why I can't afford to take the RISD scholarship: "Someone has to make a—".

Ziggy *(to Gene—figuring out "the catch")*: Yeah, yeah, but how doesh he collect *next* year if he jusht worksh three weeksh?

Gene: Here's the beauty part. I already got my twenty weeks in. So every week *I'm* on the books now, I lose a check.

Clifford *(to audience)*: This kind of talk used to drive my mother crazy.

Gene: So the *kid* works three weeks at his TV gig. Quits. Then I do club dates under *his* name, the union won't know—

Al: —*you* work seventeen weeks under his name,—

Ziggy: —*he* getsh hish twenty weeksh in—

Jonesy: —that way *you* collect—

Al: —he pays you cash for the gig you do in his name—

Gene *(to Clifford)*: You're getting your weeks, I'm—

Clifford: Dad, Dad—It's not TV, it's advertising. I don't have the job yet. I may not get it. And if I *do* get the gig, I may not quit. *(Group is appalled)* I mean, it might be worth trying to stay.

Gene *(to the guys, winking)*: I have no son.

(The guys crack up. Patsy returns, with five separate checks)

Patsy: Here you go fellas.

(Gene signals for her to give him all the checks. The men, and Patsy, stop in mid-breath)

Gene: No, no, my treat. *(To Patsy)* My boy signed for his first check today.

Patsy: Did you really? Congratulations, Gene!

(Clifford nonchalantly shrugs. Gene beams)

Patsy: Drop by later kid, I'll buy you a drink.

(Al, Ziggy, Jonesy ogle Patsy as she walks away)

Patsy: Keep it in your pants, boys.

(Gene stares at his son)

Clifford *(to audience)*: My father covers the checks, and then, he does something else he's almost never done. He looks at me. He just stops and stares. And I think he sees something, some promise, some sadness, or . . .

(*Gene starts to whistle the first phrase of* The Afternoon of a Faun. *Clifford waves a hand in front of his father's face: no reaction*)

Clifford: He's gone now. Back to when he had no son, back to 1953—before the Beatles, before Elvis. When these guys were like ball players. On the road, written up in the papers, endorsing trumpets in *Down Beat*. Bands passing each other in the night even traded side men: one first trumpet player and an alto for a second trumpet and a tenor to be named later.

(*Lights fade on the guys as they exit, and come up on a dimly-lit hotel basement—overhead pipes, low ceiling, white walls. Clifford sets up a few folding chairs.*

NOTE: *Throughout the rest of the first act, Clifford, when narrating, also stage manages, or plays caretaker to his parents and their friends. He hands or receives props, drinks, instruments, clothes, and even does simple set changes. He is engaged and in motion throughout*)

Clifford: It was after such a trade my father found himself returning to New York, to his usual room— nine dollars a week—at the Hotel Nevada, an old Upper West Side dive. Mom told me that after road trips, he'd stay there a couple of weeks, until he was clean enough to go home to his mother in the

Bronx. The Nevada let the musicians practice in the basement . . . Right now, a young flutist thinks she has the place all to herself.

(Lights up on Terry—Clifford hands a flute to a young Terry as she enters. She is twenty-four, fresh-scrubbed face, curly Italian hair. Hand-sewn clothes. She starts to play The Afternoon of a Faun. *Sweet simple tone.* **She misses a note**)

Terry: Fuck.

(Terry takes a breath, starts to play again. She gets to the same passage. Hits the same clam: Daaah-duh-dah duh daa dah. She cannot find the right note)

Terry: Fuck.

(Now from somewhere else amidst the pipes, a sweet trumpet starts the phrase again, in the flutist's key, echoing her and correcting her at the same time. Gets to the area where she's wiped out, slows down, gracefully plays through the phrase: Da-duh deee-dah. *She listens. Then picks up her flute, starts again.*

In unison now, slowly: Da-duh deee-dah. *They play together for awhile, he now starts to swing the melody. She gets to another tricky spot, wipes out. This time he quotes her wipe out, riffs on it. Starts to really improvise on the phrase)*

Terry: Fuck.

(She puts her flute down. Starts to disassemble it and put it in her case. He continues to improvise on Debussy. His sound gets jazzier.)

Terry *(to herself)*: Show off.

(Clifford stands at the bar unseen by Gene or Terry. Now Gene enters)

Gene: Name that tune.

(She looks up)

Terry: Mine or yours?

Gene: Yours.

Terry: How many seconds?

Gene *(whistles the tune again)*: As many as you want, just name it.

Terry: What do I win?

Gene *(thinking)*: A ticket to see Woody Herman?

Terry: How can you get a ticket?

Gene: Friends of mine are in the band.

Terry: You're teasing me.

Gene: You have six seconds. Five . . . four . . . three . . . t—

Terry: Time out. Stop the clock. You don't know it?

Gene: It doesn't swing.

Terry: It did when you played it.

Gene: Are you new in town?

Terry: I've been here four days, thank you.

Gene: My mistake. It's classical, right? (*Whistles first few notes again*) My mother played it when I was—

Terry: Your mother played trumpet?

Gene: No. Cello. With Casals.

Terry: Pablo?

Gene: Him too.

Terry: And you don't know it?

Gene: Only had two lessons. She caught me roller-skating with her cello. Made me study trumpet, with her father.

Terry: A jazz trumpet player?

Gene: Moscow Symphony. Tell me what it is. *Please* . . . I'll never be able to nap unless I get it out of my head.

Terry: *Afternoon of a Faun.* Debussy. (*Mispronounced: De-BOO-sy*)

(Gene is greatly relieved)

Terry: Whatever the fuck a faun is.

Gene: It's a little deer.

Terry: Ohh.

Gene: . . . dear. Useful for crosswords.

Terry *(very impressed)*: You do crosswords?

Gene: Sure.

Terry: Shit.

Gene: You know all the other four-letter words. I'm surprised you don't know fawn.

Terry: Screw you . . .

(Terry starts to walk away)

Gene: Cold front. Feel the breeze. Catch you later.

(Clifford goes to her)

Clifford: Ma—that's not how this ends . . .

Terry *(to Clifford)*: It would have been a lot easier—

Clifford: Yeah, but . . .

Terry *(to Clifford)*: All right.

(Clifford takes her flute, hands her a wrapped sandwich. Then she and Gene replay the scene from a second before)

Terry: Screw you . . .

(Terry starts to leave again, but—)

Terry: . . . dear.

(Gene turns to her. Smiles)

Gene: It's Genie.

Terry: "Genie?" Make a wish?

Gene: Genie Glimmer. Gene.

(He puts out his cuff-linked, manicured hand for her to shake)

Terry: Anna Maria Prencipe Defeceo Abbruzese.

Gene: What do they call you for short?

Terry: Crazy Terry.

Gene: Sure. Why not—

Terry: My brother Guy says I look like St. Teresa when she was hallucinating.

Gene: She wasn't hallucinating, the chick was having a major orgas—

Terry: You look like you're starving. Do you want some of this?

(She offers him her sandwich. Gene shakes his head)

Gene: I'm fine.

Terry *(maternal)*: You don't have to be embarrassed 'cause your hungry. I mean, I don't have a pot to piss in, or a window to throw it out. But you shouldn't go without eating. Here have some.

(Gene takes a huge bite out of the sandwich)

Terry: When was the last time you had something to eat?

Gene *(chewing, shameless)*: An hour ago. Bickfords. Breakfast.

Terry: Breakfast? It's three in the afternoon.

Gene: I just got back into town at six this morning—Woody's band.

Terry: You're in Woody's . . .

Gene: We're in Philly, we play 'til four, then onto the bus with my road tour pillow. *(He double-joints his arms over his head)* Now I'm trying to get some life back into my chops before tonight.

Terry: What's tonight?

Gene: The Paramount. Thanks for the sandwich.

Terry: *The* Paramount?

Gene: As far as I know.

(Gene nods, it's no big deal to him, it's unthinkably glamorous to her)

Terry: You can't *really* get me a ticket?

Gene: It'll be at the door, kid.

(Gene takes the sandwich, walks off. Terry turns to Clifford who brings her a coat and purse. Slowly, we start to hear the sound of a big swing band)

Terry *(to Clifford)*: I went.

Clifford: *He really got you a ticket?*

Terry: *He* couldn't get a ticket, so he met me at the stage door. He told me to stay in the basement—

Clifford: Classy.

Terry: —but I snuck upstairs and watched from the wings.

(We listen with Terry to the sound of a soaring trumpet section. Soloing above them now, a heartbreakingly beautiful trumpet)

Terry *(to Clifford)*: He has a beautiful tone. I went to the band room afterwards to tell him.

(Ziggy, Al, Jonesy, all younger, zoot-suited, packing up. They are in their prime. A lot of bustle except for Gene who seems to move in his own incredibly slow world. Ziggy watches him)

Jonesy: Nice blowing Genie.

Gene: Not me, it was Ziggy's charts—

Ziggy: They shound like shit until *you* sholo.

Gene: I really couldn't get anything going up there. My chops are hanging . . .

(They all looked at him)

Clifford *(to audience)*: He stole the show, and he has no idea.

Terry *(to Clifford)*: He never had any idea.

Ziggy: Hey turtle, shcrew you. We'll be over at Charlie'sh.

(The guys start to leave. Al, always on the prowl, notices Terry)

Al *(to Terry)*: Hey orphan, you want to come?

Terry *(goes to Gene)*: I'm with him.

Gene *(noticing her for the first time)*: You're still here?

Terry *(confessing)*: I snuck upstairs, and heard you, you sounded so—

Al *(to Terry, on his way out)*: Beautiful doll, if he's still packing up in half an hour, c'mon over on your own.

Jonesy *(to Al)*: Let's go Romeo, libation awaits.

Al: *(to Terry)* Ask for table 69.

(This breaks the guys up. Terry doesn't get it)

Ziggy *(about Al and Gene)*: One man'sh an octopush, the other'sh a turtle.

(They leave. Terry and Gene alone now in the band room. Clifford hands Gene his trumpet case)

Terry: Are you the turtle?

Gene *(proud)*: They did a contest, on the road, Krupa's band. They timed all the slow guys. How we ate, how long it took us to pack up, to shave. I had no idea this was going on. Some of the guys knew, were *trying* to go slow. But I still beat every-body.

(She starts to help him pack. Touches the horn to put it in the case. He swiftly takes the horn away from her)

Gene: Hey—don't touch the horn! Never touch the horn.

(He lays it in the case, as if it were glass)

Terry: You sounded beautiful out there.

Gene: That guy Al, Romeo we call him, best lead player in town. Can sight-read fly shit at 500 feet.

Terry: But you're the one who gets to solo. You know who you sound like? *(She puffs her cheeks out)* You sound like Dizzy.

Gene *(he covers her mouth)*: Don't ever say that in front of the guys.

Terry: There's something you do that he does.

Gene: Just an octave and a half lower.

Terry: You don't know how good you are. You know that?

Gene: You want to go over to Charlie's? *(She nods)* Good. Just do not mention me and Dizzy in the same sentence. I am not worthy.

(Clifford watches as Terry and Gene walk out)

Clifford: They go across the street to Charlie's Melody Lounge. Where we are now: same tablecloths, same songs on the jukebox, same smell.

(They cross over to the Melody: Neon lit, red-checked hamburger joint. There's a big round booth in the back; Al and Ziggy are already there)

Clifford: Ziggy has already bought the next morning's papers—he's obsessed with Joe McCarthy.

Ziggy *(looking up from his paper)*: Anti-shemitic bashtard.

(Terry and Gene walk to the booth. He signals the guys)

Gene: Boys, this is Terry. Terry, I'd like to introduce the trumpet section.

(Ziggy and Al now rise and do shtick)

Al *(to Ziggy)*: I'm Al.

Ziggy *(to Al)*: I'm Ziggy.

Al and Ziggy *(to each other)*: How do you do?

(They shake each others' hands, then they sit back down. Patsy now arrives with drinks)

Patsy *(to Terry)*: And I'm Patsy, Romeo's piece on the side.

Ziggy *(pointing to Al's toupée)*: Not to be con-fewshed with hish piece on top.

(Everyone makes a face at this. Ziggy shrugs)

Patsy: What are you drinking?

Terry: Water's OK.

Patsy: Water? Genie, another one out for your money. What do you do, meet these girls the moment they step off the boat?

Ziggy: Order a drink honey, itsh polite. *(About Patsy)* She'sh putting hershelf through medical shchool. One intern at a time.

Terry *(has no idea what's going on)*: I'll have a ...

Patsy and Terry: Shirley Temple.

(Patsy goes off-stage as Jonesy now lurches into the booth)

Ziggy: Incoming!

(Jonesy has evidently shot up, Terry is worried by his state, the others take it completely in stride. He passes out, slowly, face flat on the table)

Ziggy *(makes an umpire's call)*: Shafe!

Terry: Is he OK?

Gene: Honey, he's fine. He just likes to . . . relax after a gig.

(Terry is oblivious to the cause of his condition, but she is concerned)

Terry: He doesn't look so good.

Ziggy: He doeshn't feel sho bad—

Terry *(in Jonesy's ear)*: What did you eat today? Did you have tuna? I bet you had tuna, mayonnaise— you have to be very careful in warm weather.

(She lifts Jonesy's head off the table. Al and Ziggy are laughing. She takes a napkin, dips it in water, wipes his brow)

Terry *(to Jonesy, loud)*: Was it tuna? Does anything hurt?

Jonesy *(nods back in for a second)*: Jesus, Gene, you didn't tell me you were dating Florence Nightingale.

(He nods back out)

(Over to the bar, where Patsy, dressed in the coat she wore at the beginning of the play, enters and resumes her 1985 talk with Clifford. Music goes back to I Remember Clifford last heard when Clifford entered the Melody Lounge)

Patsy: How's Terry?

Clifford: Good days, bad days—

Patsy: Old days. She was something else back then, Clifford.

(Patsy and Clifford look across the stage to the booth: They watch Terry take the lit cigarette out of Jonesy's hand and put it out. He doesn't notice)

Clifford *(to Patsy)*: She still has her moments: just got kicked out of her senior center crafts course for crochetting obscene homilies.

Patsy: I tried calling, but she—

Clifford: She doesn't talk to too many people.

Patsy: Everyone always turns on Terry. You know your father and I never—

Clifford: Even if you did, he wouldn't have noticed.

Patsy: Don't be mean, you. *(Listens to the music)* He's playing *I Remember Clifford*.

Clifford: Genie on a ballad—break your heart every time.

(She kisses him on the cheek—music out, lights cross fade as Clifford helps Patsy take off her coat. She leaves him and crosses the stage, over to the booth, drinks in hand. It's 1953 again)

Patsy: I'm off for a while.

(She sits on Al's lap, while he finishes rolling a joint)

Gene: So's Jonesy.

Terry: I think he may have had some bad tuna. He doesn't look very good.

Patsy: Wait a few minutes . . .

Ziggy: He'll look worshe.

(While they've been talking, Al and the guys have started passing the joint. He passes it to Patsy)

Terry: You roll your own? I should do that. It's much more economical.

Patsy *(to Gene, while taking a hit off the joint)***:** Is she for real?

(The joint is passed from Al, to Ziggy, to Gene, to Terry, who, thinking it's a cigarette, takes a drag. Keeps up her nervous monologue)

Terry: I don't smoke that much. The only reason I started smoking at all was because the sisters at St. Mary's accused me of smoking all the time, so I finally figured I'd start smoking—Pall Mall Golds, 'cause that's what my brother Guy, he's a narcotics agent, *(Ziggy, Al, Gene and even Jonesy cough on this. Terry doesn't miss a beat)* smoked; although nobody ever accused him of smoking. And I've seen people roll their own in the movies, but aren't you clever for rolling your own like this. And then, the way you all share—(*Hands the joint to Gene*) here . . .

Patsy: What planet did you come from?

Terry: Baltimore. Not originally. East Boston originally, but I can't go back because my husband, Dominic Defeces, the brick-laying prick, just left me, in Baltimore. I wrote Blimpie, she's my oldest sister, there's seven others, that I had to come home, and she wrote me and told me, "Don't come back." 'Cause my mother, Italian, Catholic, thinks divorce is a sin—even though the rat-bastard got an annulment to run off with my best friend, she'll make me join a fuckin' convent in Montana, if I do. Go home. So Blimpie, Cupie, Fat Raffie and some of my other sisters pitched in and sent me a money tree with twenty-five dollars. So I came to New York. The room's eight, so now I'm down to thirteen dollars, but I can't go home. But I'm not worried because—

Ziggy: Anybody following thish?

Jonesy (*looks up from his haze*): I am.

Al: What's she saying?

Jonesy: Her prick husband, a mudslinger, took her from East Boston, which is a fuckin' tough ghetto, let me tell you, and left her in Baltimore. But Italians don't divorce—so she had to come here. Good-night now. *(He nods back out)*

Ziggy: You're in luck then. Jazz musiciansh divorce all the time. Patshy'sh on her third trumpet player.

Terry: You and Al are married?

Patsy: No. I mean, I am, he's not. My husband's on the road.

Ziggy: Romeo'sh what you call the relief band. Shpeaking of which, we're due downtown in 0 *(looks at watch)* twenty minutesh ago.

Patsy: And I'm back in . . .

Al: We'll hop a cab, *(to Ziggy)* your treat.

Ziggy *(grabbing Jonesy off the table)*: I'll have to roll Joneshy. Genie, you coming?

Gene: I'll catch up with you later.

Terry *(as the gang leaves)*: Nice to meet you all. *(To Gene)* It's amazing how economical you all are.

(Terry holds the remains of the joint but since it's now roach size, and since she thinks it's a cigarette, she just puts it out in an ashtray)

Terry: It's pretty much down to the end. Here, have one of mine.

(Gene watches in shock Now Gene takes Terry's hand and leads her out of the bar, and across the stage.)

Clifford: They didn't make it downtown that night, instead he took her to his room in the Hotel Nevada, for a nightcap. That's when she saw . . .

(Lights up on a bare room, as Terry and Gene enter)

Terry *(to Gene, now in his room)*: **You have a sink?**

Gene: State of the art—cold comes out of the hot, cold comes out of the cold—

(Terry looks at the photos on the wall)

Terry: Is that you with Frank Sinatra?

Gene: When he comes to town, he usually adds me to his—

Terry: Oh my God, I've wanted to see him my whole life. More than anything.

Gene: Next time he's here, I'll get you in.

(Clifford hands him a wire-recorder. Gene fiddles with it)

Terry: Wait a minute, you're bullshitting me. Right? Everyone always does that. You didn't really play with him, did—

Gene: Here, this is me with him at the Copa—recorded it from backstage on this very wire recorder.

(*A choppy quality, but recognizable Sinatra bootleg, live from the Copa. A trumpet section soars behind Sinatra. They listen for a few bars*)

Terry: That's so beautiful.

Gene: The club manager caught me with it, picked up the whole wire recorder, threw it against the wall. It still plays. We were gonna write to the company, see if they'd do an endorsement ad. "Famed Copa Manager and Hoodlum Jules Podell Couldn't Break This, Neither Will You."

(*They listen for a few moments. Terry goes to Gene. She grabs his hand*)

Terry: Do you want to dance? With me?

Gene: Trumpet players don't dance—bad for the chops. Come here, let's just listen.

(*He takes her in his arms. They kiss, as the voice of Sinatra comes up, and the lights fade down*)

Clifford: That night, with the help of Frank Sinatra, they made love. Then slept together, very close, in a single bed with the blinking neon of the Hotel Nevada flickering off and on.

(*He watches them sleep as the lights fade up*)

Clifford: Morning comes, and Terry's a little more chipper than he is.

Terry *(to Gene)***:** Do you want to live together?

(He jumps)

Gene: I'm going on the road in a couple of weeks. Maybe sooner.

Terry: I'll find us a place while you're gone. When you come back, it will be all fixed up.

Gene: No—it's out of the—

(Terry moves into their new apartment. Gene, in shock, tries to move quickly after her. But even when he moves quickly he's slow. The doorbell rings)

Terry: We're in here!

(Ziggy, Al, and Jonesy arrive with furniture, from busted marriages, for the next scene; Gene remains in the last scene, or a limbo, for a little while)

Ziggy *(with Al, carrying a couch)***:** The Sheven Shantini are here, minush four.

Al: Where do you want this?

(Jonesy unrolls a rug onto the floor)

Ziggy: We were going to let Al carry the rug, but he already hash one.

(Terry supervises as Gene exits. And, like that—they're moved in. Terry shows Al, Ziggy, and Jonesy where everything goes; she rearranges things)

Al: Hey, Terry. Nice crib.

Terry: There's a crib coming?

Jonesy: Four-letter word baby.

Terry *(getting it)*: Ohhh.

Ziggy *(struggling to find something to compliment)*: The floorsh look good.

(Jonesy walks in with a lamp. Al plugs it in, as Terry embarks on another monologue)

Terry: I did them by hand. I fucked-up my fingers something awful. Then I made the curtains out of some tablecloths I stole from Charlie's. You know, those nice red and white ones. I went in, had a coffee, and I started pulling the thing off the table. Patsy looks at me, and says, "What are you doing?" So I says to her, "I'm stealing a tablecloth to make curtains, what does it look like?" She came back with three more tablecloths in a paper bag, "Here," she says, "the new manager is a prick."

(Al and Ziggy have no idea what she's talking about. Jonesy followed her perfectly. She exits to kitchen. The guys are alone)

Al *(sotto voce)*: So dig this guys—It's four A.M., I'm in my bed, there's a knock at the door. I open it, there's this beautiful blond in a full-length mink coat. She says, "Are you Al Paradisio?" I say, "Baby, I'm anyone you want me to be." She pops open da mink—nuttin' on—"Happy Birthday," she says, "From Charlie Barnett."

Ziggy: Cockshucker gave me cuff linksh.

(Now Gene walks in cradling an oversized non-descript box that he seems to believe is very delicate)

Gene: Hey guys, check it out.

Al: Whoa. Easy does it, let it down nice and easy.

Gene: I copped it from Leon.

Terry *(entering)*: What is that thing?

Gene: It's an orgone box.

Terry: Orgone? Like the Japanese POWs used to do? After the war I worked at a holding camp and—

Ziggy: What ish she talking about—

Jonesy *(gently explaining)*: That's origami, this is orgone.

Ziggy: How come he undershtandsh her?

Gene: Orgone box—Wilhelm Reich designed it.

Al *(to Gene)*: Does she know about Reich?

Terry: What did he play?

(This cracks Ziggy and Jonesy up. Now Al lights a joint. NOTE: They are all pretty close to high to begin with, so they get stoned quickly. On the other hand, they're pretty used to being stoned, so it's not like they're seeing colors or anything)

Gene: Wilhelm Reich. Shrink, writes about . . . *(takes the joint, inhales)*

Al: . . . about the armor that people carry on themselves.

(Al passes the joint to Terry, who still smokes it like a cigarette)

Al: . . . it's caused by sexual repression, from the society, the family, and it causes people to develop . . . armor. Which they think protects them—

Jonesy: Honey, can you pass that?

(She takes one more drag on the joint, coughs)

Terry: You guys get the shittiest tobacco.

Al: —but, you see, what the armor really does is shut them off from just . . . fucking freely without shame. *(In mid-toke)* Now you see good sex, I'm talking *really* good sex—*(Finishes toke)*

Ziggy: Like with shomeone who'sh awake—

(The others look at him)

Al: —really good sex, releases orgones. Which are this positive energy. And that box collects those orgones.

Gene: That's what this box does.

Terry: You guys are fucking weird.

Jonesy: Put your hand inside.

Terry: What?

Ziggy: You shaid you hurt your hand, shcraping the floorsh, right? Jusht put your hand inshide.

(Terry's not sure what to do)

Gene: Go ahead. It's OK.

(She does)

Jonesy: I can't believe Leon's old lady wouldn't let him keep his box.

Gene: His old lady's moving him to Massachusetts.

Ziggy: Who'sh he gonna play with in Masha, Mashaschu—fuck it, Boshton.

Al: What play? She wants him out of the business.

Jonesy: Leon? Neon Leon? Tell me he could get a job other than playing trumpet.

Terry: Who's Neon Leon?

Gene: Neon Leon. I told you about him. The one Benny Goodman fired because he peed on stage.

Jonesy (*as Leon, stage whispers*)**:** *"Benny, Benny—I gotta go."*

Al (*as Benny Goodman*)**:** *"That's not my problem, Neon, you knew about this gig weeks ago."*

Jonesy: *"Benny, what am I supposed to do?"*

Al: *"You can pee on the stage for all I care."*

Ziggy: Sho he did.

Al: He's a motherfucker though. Let's face it, he's a motherfucker.

(*The guys all agree, he's a motherfucker*)

Jonesy: Total motherfucker.

Terry: Is motherfucker good or bad?

Jonesy *(gently explaining)*: G's above high C, all night long.

Gene: What a waste, chops like that, going to law school.

Ziggy: We oughtta have a wake: Requiem for a Motherfucker.

(Lights dim on them, lights up on Clifford, as a funeral march, Louis Armstrong's St. James Infirmary, *plays)*

Clifford *(to audience)*: A moment of silence. For Leon. Since he's leaving the business, in effect, he's passed away. Over the years there'd be more and more of these moments. Guys would O.D., or go to jail, or worse get married and have to work 9 to 5. By the time I was on the scene, these guys were sort of an underground railroad to the straight world. We got our eyeglasses from a former tenor player, car insurance from an alto, and of course that box, from Leon.

(Back to the living room, music out)

Jonesy: How's your hand?

Terry: What?

Jonesy: Your hand.

(She takes it out of the box. Stares at it)

Terry: Holy shit. It's better. It's almost healed.

Jonesy: HALLELUJAH.

Terry *(scared)*: What the fuck is in there?

Ziggy and Al *(spooky-voice)*: *Orrrr-gooones.*

Gene: Don't ever tell anyone we have one of these things. They're illegal. They're chasing Reich all over the country.

Terry: You guys are fuckin' weird. I don't want that thing in my house. Get it out.

Gene: Calm down, Terry. It's harmless.

Terry: I'm serious, get it out.

Ziggy: Wait 'til she shee's the resht of Leon's shtuff.

(Terry, very quickly, loses it. She starts to beat Gene's chest with her hands. He grabs them)

Terry: Don't tease me. I hate when you all do that.

Gene: Terry, no one is doing anything to you.

Terry *(embarrassed, calming down)*: OK—still, get it out of the house.

Jonesy *(going to the door)*: C'mon guys. Let's—

Al: I want to stay and watch.

Ziggy: C'mon, Al.

(They leave. Gene goes to her, holds her. Calms her down)

Terry: Is that thing really illegal?

Gene: Nobody knows what it is, so we can't get in trouble.

Terry: Do we have to have it in the house?

Gene: I'll take care of it.

(She calms down. Patsy enters at the booth of the Melody Lounge. Terry crosses to her)

Patsy: So, what's the problem?

Terry: Gene's got some box. He says it's illegal. And it collects oregons that—

Patsy: Orgones. Leon used to have one.

Terry *(happy this story checks out)***:** That's where Genie got it.

Patsy: Leon's old lady probably made him give it up. She made him give everything else up—which is more than I ever got him to do.

Terry: You went out with Neon Leon?

Patsy: Neon was my first husband. Not that he'd remember. The Big Junked-Out Lug. I told him, "If you really become a lawyer, I'll let you handle all my divorces."

Terry: I couldn't make it through another divorce. When Dominic left me, I thought I'd go crazy.

Patsy: They get easier. After a while, it's like falling off a bicycle.

Terry: That rat-bastard—left me for my best friend. You and Genie never—

Patsy *(laughs)***:** Oh, honey. No. Never. I promise.

Terry: Leon wasn't really a junkie, was he?

Patsy: Doll, you don't have to worry about that with Gene. Gene's clean. He's the one they all call when their cars break down.

(Terry nods, without really following this)

Clifford *(to audience)***:** This was some sort of code, 'cause these guys' cars always break, *(to Terry, winking)* and half of them don't even have cars.

(Clifford hands her a dinner tray with two soup bowls she crosses to the living room)

Clifford *(to audience)***:** It took a while, but Mom started to get the gist of Patsy's field work on trumpet players.

(*Back to the apartment, a quiet dinner. Terry serves Gene. He eats slowly, blows on his soup*)

Terry: Patsy says these doo-wop groups don't even use horns.

(*Gene shakes his head at this*)

Gene: She's married three trumpet players in a row, so she must think there's some future in it.

Terry: She says the big bands are gone for good. And a lot of the clubs are—

Gene: Terry, trust me, it's nothing to worry about. I'm a professional. Like a doctor, or a lawyer. And here in New York, with all the TV and radio here. You can't ask for a more secure field—every station will have to have its own band. Honest.

Terry: Then why is Patsy's husband getting out?

Gene: That's her *ex*-husband. The second one. Stu. Not Bernie. Bernie's a motherfucker—he's out on the road sixty weeks a year. When he comes back to town, Charlie Barnett's gonna add him to the band, and we'll record.

Terry: Then why is Stu getting out?

Gene: Stu's a lead player. Great chops, but he can only work the big bands. But I'm a true side man— I can solo, back up a singer—

Terry: Or fake Deboosy—

Gene: And harmony. Three part. Four part. I'm a
. . . a—

Terry: A jack-of-all-trades.

Gene: Bingo.

(They kiss, then she pulls back)

Terry: Wait—it wasn't just Stu—Al too. She said he
hasn't even had a Saturday night this month.

Gene: That won't happen. To me. I mean, look: if
there ever comes a Saturday night, when I'm not
booked, just one Saturday night, then—I promise,
I'll get out of the business, OK?

Terry: You don't have to say that.

Gene: But I can. It's the easiest promise I could ever
make.

(She kisses him)

Terry: Are you going to be on the road a lot?

Gene: I used to think I was. But you came in and
(looks around) . . .

Terry: You like it?

Wendy Makkena *(left)* as Terry and Frank Wood as Gene. All photographs of the 1998 Roundabout Theater Company production by Carol Rosegg.

Left to right: Angelica Torn, Frank Wood, Michael Mastro, Joseph Lyle Taylor, Kevin Geer, and Robert Sella in the Roundabout Theatre Company production of the *Side Man*.

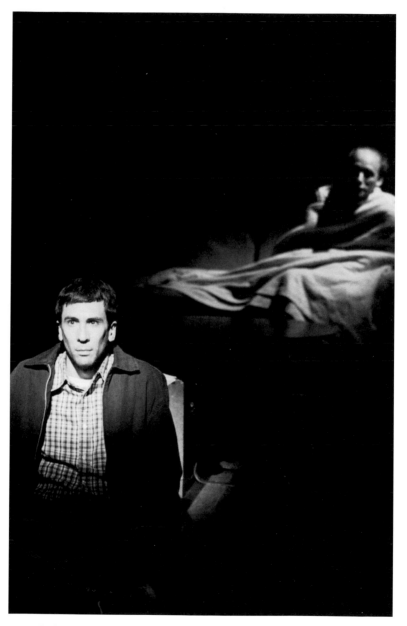

Robert Sella *(left)* as Clifford and Frank Wood as Gene.

Michael Mastro *(left)* as Ziggy, Frank Wood as Gene and Joseph Lyle Taylor as Al.

Gene: I've never had a home in my life—I like it a lot.

Terry: Patsy's gonna get me a job waitressing soon, at Charlie's. So you won't have to—

Gene: No. I don't want you working. I'm a little behind now—with the car breaking down, and the rent—but we're almost out of the woods. And (*looks straight into her eyes*), I promise you. I'm going to take care of us, (*kisses her*) you won't ever have to work at all.

(*Terry stands*)

Terry: (*yelling to a kitchen's short-order window*): BLT please, whiskey down.

(*From the other side of the stage now, Patsy, in a waitress uniform, meets Terry downstage, hands her an apron*)

Patsy (*to an unseen cook*): Fry two, in butter please, *not* grease. Thank you. (*To Terry*) The prick at table six is waving for you.

Terry: He tries to cop a feel every time I refill his coffee.

Patsy: If he does it again, spill some on his lap. How's Genie? (*To cook*) Can I have my eggs please?

Terry: He's going to record, with Charlie Barnett. He says after that we should be squared away.

Patsy *(subtle announcement)*: Are you gonna come to my wedding?

Terry: Patsy—that's great! *(She gives Patsy a big hug, then:)* Who are you marrying?

Patsy: *Al.* I've been in love with him since Leon and I were engaged.

Terry: Good for you.

Patsy *(to cook)*: Where the fuck are my eggs?

Terry: Does Al mind you waitressing?

Patsy: Somebody has to make a living.

Terry: Genie can't stand it. He says—

Patsy: He'll get used to it—they all do.

(Over to Clifford, at the bar; while he speaks, the guys return to the apartment, with ever more stuff. They place an end table down, upside down. Its bottom shelf now at top. Ziggy looks at the end table. Something's wrong)

Ziggy *(to Jonesy)*: Shomething'sh wrong.

(Now they see the problem. Pick it up and clock it 180 degrees, still upside down, however)

Ziggy and Jonesy: Aaaahhh.

(They go back outside for more stuff. NOTE: *Throughout the rest of the play, the portion of the stage that is their apartment will go from bare to full to cluttered to cramped: Mismatched furniture, slightly broken or chipped chairs, frayed carpet)*

Clifford: While the rest of the country was moving to the suburbs, Mom and Dad stayed in the city. Nine floors up. Rent controlled. Little by little their place filled up. The apartment became "the hang out" before I was born. The lamps were from Ziggy's first marriage.

(Ziggy enters with two lamps)

Terry *(to herself)*: Sweet kid, what was her name?

(She joins Clifford at the bar. Gene sits on the couch, ignoring her)

Ziggy: Shushie.

Terry *(to Clifford)*: Right. Susie—then he broke up with her, and dated . . . Cecelia?

Ziggy: Sheshily.

(Ziggy leaves. Terry continues with Clifford)

Terry: I told Ziggy: "Date someone whose name you can pronounce. Lana. Diane."

Clifford *(to audience)*: When Patsy finally divorced Bernie to marry Al, we . . . they (I'm not on the scene yet) got Bernie's stuff.

(Patsy and Al come on—lovebirds for the moment. She carries a box of Bernie's records, mariachas, and bongos. Al carries Bernie's hi-fi)

Patsy *(to Terry)*: Ziggy's moving in with Sheshily. Get this: Sheventy Shecond Shtreet.

Al *(to the girls)*: It'll never last. She's a call girl.

Terry *(doesn't get the problem)*: What's wrong with working for an answering service?

Patsy: It's doomed—they'll each want the other to get out of the business.

Terry *(to Clifford)*: Patsy was right. Ziggy went back on the road. We got his hi-fi.

(Gene stays in his own world on the couch. Jonesy comes in, carrying a TV set, placed center stage. Ziggy brings a six-pack of beer. Patsy and Al neck—for a moment. Then she stops. Slaps him)

Terry: Then, six months after they got married, Patsy and Al split up, and we got Al's TV set. And Al for a couple of months—on Bernie's couch.

(Jonesy and Ziggy move Al, as if he were another hand-me-down, onto the couch. Patsy plugs in the TV)

Patsy: This was almost my TV. Twice.

(Terry and Patsy exit. Gene, Al, Ziggy and Jonesy sit, and watch TV. Ziggy passes out a six-pack, looks at the furnishings)

Ziggy: Genie, the Shalvation Army ish ready to talk peace—

Gene *(to the guys)*: I tell Terry, our apartment is furnished in Early American Divorce.

(The guys break up at this. Terry returns with plates of food. Patsy turns on the hi-fi. A party tableau: Patsy dances with Ziggy. A 1950s conga line starts: Ziggy, Patsy, Gene, Terry, Al—and finally Jonesy—playing bongos at the rear of the line.

In the living room, everyone freezes. A flash goes off: A HAPPY TIMES PHOTO. They are captured on film in one final happy moment)

Clifford *(looks at photos from long ago, looks in the living room at the party)*: From what I understand, EVERYTHING WAS HAPPY BEFORE I WAS BORN.

(Everyone looks at Clifford, then—)

Patsy: He's on!

(—the line splits up. All grab seats to watch the TV)

Terry: They're only showing him from the waist up. They're scared shitless.

Clifford *(to audience)*: This would be the night Elvis first played the *Ed Sullivan Show*.

(Group, this time including Patsy, who's now arm-in-arm with Ziggy, watches Elvis on TV. Jonesy stares intensely at the screen. Hound Dog ends to TV cheers, Jonesy turns the set off)

Jonesy: Anybody here know how to play guitar?

(Gene, Ziggy, Al shake their heads)

Jonesy: Too bad. That kid will do to horn players what talkies did to Buster Keaton. Mark my words.

(They all look at him. Terry is the only one who doesn't laugh. Al follows Jonesy as he leaves)

Terry *(to Clifford)*: Jonesy got arrested that night. Your father told me he got plastered and they took away his cabaret card, for disorderly conduct, which meant he couldn't work in New York, and we got his coffee table.

(Al puts the coffee table in front of the couch. Ziggy and Patsy, who are necking on the couch, put their plates down on it without losing a beat, then exit after Al. Clifford hands Terry a postcard)

Terry: He moved to Vegas for the year. Said it was wide open and *(to Gene)* WE SHOULD COME DOWN.

Gene: Las Vegas? It's in the middle of a desert.

Terry: Jonesy's doing well there, and he plays trombone. I have a feeling that—

Gene: You run the kitchen, let me take care of business. Vegas is never gonna—there's no future in it. It's a mirage.

Terry (*while clearing plates and bottles to kitchen*): What about L.A.? Ziggy says some of the TV shows are moving there.

Gene: Terry—it won't happen. New York is where the work is, and always will be.

Clifford (*from the bar*): Gene was sort of an antipsychic. But Mom was raised to believe papa knew best. And Pops was a City College man, after all. Besides, by now, Gene and Ziggy had gotten the idea that they could make it big as comedy writers for the Sid Ceasar show.

(*Clifford hands Gene and Ziggy two scripts. They pace back and forth, scripts in hand, working on their comedy routine. Terry watches*)

Ziggy (*reading the script, in the voice of a British Queen*): "Damnation, *shays the Queen*, the Duke goeth down not before I, hish Royal Highnessh?"

Gene (*mock British*): "He giveth no Crown? Wouldst her ladyship prefer him beheaded or . . . hung?"

Ziggy (*reading the Queen*): "You fool, if he'd been hung in the firsht place, he wouldsh't not need hish head at all."

(They laugh themselves silly; then leave. Terry watches them go)

Terry *(to Clifford)*: They must have spent a hundred hours on those scripts. But they never sent them out.

(Patsy, with two drinks in hand, meets the twenty-one-year-old Clifford, in a booth at Charlie's. It is 1977)

Patsy: Here you go, Clifford. In honor of your first unemployment check. Cheers.

Clifford: Thanks.

Patsy: And these are for you too.

(She drops an envelope on the table, stuffed with papers)

Clifford: What are they?

Patsy: Gene told me you're going to study TV, in Rhode Island. And I remembered, I still had some of his and Ziggy's scripts, I thought maybe you could—

Clifford: No, Genie gets it . . . wrong. I got a scholarship for Art School, in Rhode Island.

Patsy: Ohh. Well, congratulations on that. I could have sworn Gene said TV.

Clifford: It's not TV, it's advertising. It's this job I'm up for. In New York.

Patsy: Here's to you—in *Rhode Island.*

Clifford: The advertising job would pay really well and—

Patsy: You don't need money, you're a kid.

Clifford: *I* don't need anything, but Gene's so far behind on his credit cards—

Patsy: Genie is always behind—

Clifford: And Mom's not doing so well, lately. Her health . . .

(Patsy, very sober all of a sudden, looks at Clifford)

Patsy: Why do you think that is?

Clifford: I'm sorry?

Patsy: Clifford, when you were about to go away to college, the same thing happened.

Clifford: It's a good thing I didn't go away to college. Can you imagine Genie handling the—

Patsy: Clifford, listen to me: I don't care what you do, or where you go—just get the hell out of here.

(Gene and Terry enter from bedroom door—a serious discussion underway. Clifford watches)

Gene: Are you sure?

Terry: It's been two months.

Gene: Al knows someone who can take care of it.

Terry: What?

Gene: Patsy knows him too, he's very—

Terry (*horrified*): What are you talking about?

Gene: Terry, you're not in East Boston anymore. You don't have to have a baby just because—

Terry: You want to kill the baby? Our baby? OK, OK. It's OK.

Gene (*goes to her*): Terry—there's no baby yet.

Terry: Oh my God. Oh my God. Oh my God.

Gene: The sooner you take care of these things, the better it—

Terry: Shut up. SHUT UP. SHUT UP. I don't want to kill the baby. I wanna have the baby. I don't care if he's a bastard. I want to keep the baby.

Gene: Terry. Calm down. Get a—he won't be a bastard.

(*She calms down, a bit*)

Gene: Terry . . . we're getting married. OK? You're having the baby. It's OK. It's OK.

Terry: You mean it?

Gene: Sure.

Terry: Oh, Genie.

(They embrace, then she pulls back)

Terry: You know, I've already been married.

Gene: We'll do it 'til you get it right. *(They kiss)* We'll have a big wedding. I'll take care of everything. In the morning I'll talk to the caterers.

Terry: We can't afford that. I can cook a lasagne—

Gene: Terry, it's your wedding. We'll have a band, a cake, the works. This is going to be a night to remember.

(Gene exits, to plan the celebration)

Terry *(to Clifford)*: That was that. Two weeks later—

(Clifford crosses downstage to Terry)

Clifford: You made a lasagne.

Terry: And we got married—

Clifford and Terry: In the apartment.

(Clifford helps her out of her robe—underneath, a wedding dress. She puts on shoes and a ring. He adds a corsage)

Terry: I called Blimpie, Cupie, Fat Raffie, all my sisters, but they couldn't come . . . Afterwards, we went over to Charlie's to celebrate. Jonesy—he'd just gotten back from Vegas, danced with me while Gene sat in with the band. Everyone cut in all night long. Not to dance with me, but to sit in with Gene and the band.

(Jonesy dances with Terry to a romantic ballad played by Gene)

Terry: How come he doesn't dance with me? On his wedding night?

Jonesy: Trumpet players don't dance.

Terry: How come you dance?

Jonesy: I play trombone. Patsy taught me. After she left Al . . . before she went back to her second husband.

Terry: Bernie?

Jonesy: No. Bernie was number three. She wouldn't leave me and Al for Bernie, because Bernie still plays. Greatest lead player in America. She went back to Stu—number two, if you're keeping score. Which in Patsy's case is almost impossible to do.

Terry: Stu the foot doctor?

Jonesy (*to himself*)**:** Stu the foot doctor. (*To Terry*) He used to be a good player. He came by 52nd Street one night, saw us all play. He started to cry. Ziggy looks at him and says: "Podiatrisht, heel thyshelf."

(*The ballad ends. Jonesy and Terry applaud. She motions for Gene to come join her. Instead, the band starts another tune: like* Dahoud, *an up-tempo, undanceable hard-bop number*)

Terry: How do you dance to this?

Jonesy: You don't. You drink to it. That's another reason why jazz is dying. Let's go to the bar.

(*He steers her to the bar*)

Terry: I'll have a Shirley Temple.

Jonesy: Terry, you marry a musician, you're gonna have to learn to drink hard stuff. Start with a Tom Collins.

(*Clifford serves Terry her first drink. She and Jonesy listen to the band*)

Jonesy: Gene sounds pretty good tonight.

Terry: He told me never to tell anyone, but I think he sounds like Dizzy.

Jonesy: In a way. Nicer tone than Dizzy. But he does those same long lines. Every solo has a beginning, middle, and end when he plays.

Terry: Do you think he'll make it?

Jonesy: Honey. He's made it. This is it.

(Terry looks around, lets this sink in. Then:)

Terry: What about that record he did . . . with Charlie Barnett's band?

Jonesy: He's a player Terry. He's not a hustler.

Terry: But he played really well on it.

Jonesy: Didn't he tell you what happened?

Terry: No.

Jonesy: Ask him about the review.

Terry *(to Clifford)*: I had a nice time dancing with Jonesy. And the Tom Collins tasted kind of sweet. He bought me a few more, but then he had to leave—

Jonesy: Got to see a man about some horse. I'll be back in half an hour.

(Jonesy, who now needs a fix, has been compulsively scratching himself more and more throughout the scene. He walks out)

Clifford: An hour went by, Charlie's was closing up, and Jonesy hadn't come back. Mom, who actually was a little psychic, told Gene . . .

(Gene enters; she goes to him)

Terry: He said he was going to see some horse or something. But I don't think the race tracks are still open. Maybe something happened to him at the track—

Gene: Jonesy can take care of himself.

(Al comes by)

Al: Terry, best wishes. Genie, nice blowing tonight.

(Ziggy comes by now, with Patsy on his arm. Al tenses up)

Ziggy *(in Al's face)*: "Love ish lovelier . . .

Patsy and Ziggy *(sing)*: . . . the sheventh time around."

Patsy: Congratulations you kids.

Terry: Have you guys seen Jonesy? I'm a little worried.

Patsy and Ziggy *(sing)*: "If you knew Jonesy, like I knew Jonesy."

(Al is not having fun)

Al: Mazel tov.

Ziggy: Geshundheit.

Al: Screw you.

(Al leaves. Ziggy looks at Patsy, she shrugs)

Patsy: That stage should be over by now. Good-night everybody. Got to get home before the foot man wakes up for work.

(Patsy exits. The others now walk out of Charlie's too. End of the evening)

Terry *(to Clifford)*: When we got outside, there was a police car parked across the street. Lights flashing. In the back seat, hands cuffed behind his back, was Jonesy.

Clifford *(to audience)*: Mom spent the rest of her wedding night down in night court. Waiting.

(Gene, Ziggy, and Terry watch and wait)

Terry: How come they keep arresting Jonesy?

Ziggy: Probably another bullshit crackdown caushe shome dealer misshed hish pay-off.

(Gene signals Ziggy to shut up)

Terry: What's that have to do with Jonesy?

Gene: Look, everything's going to be fine. We can post bail. I've got . . . fourteen bucks.

Ziggy: Bragger.

Gene: Terry, you don't have to hang around.

Terry *(her feelings hurt)*: I'll stay.

(They stand and wait for a while)

Terry: Jonesy told me to ask you about the Charlie Barnett review.

Ziggy *(to Gene)*: Try to bail a guy out, and he ratsh on you.

(Gene tries to shush Ziggy)

Terry: What happened?

Gene: Didn't I tell you about this? I could have sworn I did.

Ziggy *(trying to distract)*: You guysh shee what'sh going on in Budapesht?

(Terry glares at him, turns to Gene)

Terry: What happened? And don't bullshit me.

Gene: This big French jazz critic, Henri Arnaud, reviewed the album. He said that while the band sounded great, the trumpet solos were the best in the last decade.

Terry: You're kidding. Why didn't you tell me? We should make photostats of the review. Send them out to club owners. To managers. Maybe Gene could get someone to— (*She notices they've gone silent*) You were lying to me? You fuck. Why—

Gene: No I wasn't. Honest. They liked my playing.

Ziggy: Liked it? They were nutsh about it.

Terry: Why the fuck do you two lie to me like this?

Gene: No one's lying, Terry. They liked my playing. Only problem is, they didn't know it was my playing. The guy screwed the credits up. He saw Bernie's name and everybody over there knows Bernie, because he's recorded with Miles and Gil and everyone else. It's no big deal.

Terry: What's the magazine going to do about the mistake?

Gene: I don't think they even know about it. You know, Bernie's a great player, and he deserves a good review.

Terry: NOT FOR YOUR FUCKING SOLOS HE DOESN'T.

Gene: LOWER YOUR VOICE. We're in a court for crissakes.

Terry: YOU'VE GOT TO WRITE AND TELL THEM TO MAKE A CORRECTION.

Gene: Calm down. That's not how it works. People in the business know my playing. I can't embarrass Bernie with a letter like that. (*Patronizing*) What's the matter with you?

(*She is embarrassed now. After a long awkward moment, Ziggy sees:*)

Ziggy: Joneshy. There he ish. JONESHY.

Gene: JONESY!

Terry: Oh my God! (*Waves to him*) What's the matter with him?

Ziggy: He probably needsh a fix, poor bashtard.

Terry: What do we do?

Gene: We could call Leon.

Ziggy: Leon? Nobody'sh shpoken to him shince he moved to Boshton.

Gene: He's a Harvard lawyer now. One call from a guy like that and the D.A. drops the charges.

Clifford: Leon did what he could. It took two days because it was a weekend, but on Monday, Gene got in to see Jonesy.

(Gene face-to-face with a badly beaten, strung-out Jonesy. Clifford watches intently)

Gene: Anything I can do for you?

Jonesy: Yeah, take my place.

Gene: I'm serious—

Jonesy: I'm all fucked up, Gene.

Gene: What the hell happened?

Jonesy: They wanted me to tell them who my dealer was. They said we'll give you a fix, if you tell us where you cop. They waved it in front of my face. I was dying for it. But I said, I can't trust you guys. Let me fix myself up first, then I'll tell you where I cop. So the bastards give me my stash, they'd already taken half of it for themselves, but I tie off, I shoot up, and I'm feeling no pain. OK wise ass, they say, tell us where this heroin comes from? I look them right in the eye and I tell them the truth: *(pause)* General MacArthur.

(Gene looks at Jonesy, shakes his head)

Jonesy: Well, how the hell do you think this stuff gets into the country? Anyway, this fuckin' bull goes nuts. He smacks me across the face. The other guys let him whale on me for awhile before they pulled him off. *(Jonesy opens his mouth, shows Gene his teeth)*

Jonesy: He broke three of my teeth Gene. (*Starts to cry*) I don't know if I'll ever be able to play.

(*Jonesy staggers off as Gene moves to living room. Terry knits. Clifford hands a pregnant, cigarette smoking Terry her drink*)

Clifford (*to audience*): They put him away . . . for eight years.

Terry (*to Clifford*): I wrote to him and sent care packages . . . I never heard from him.

(*Terry sits with Gene on the couch. She sips her Tom Collins. Clifford has, over the last few scenes, moved closer to the action. Now he stands in the living room and watches*)

Terry (*to Gene*): You lied to me. When Jonesy was arrested the first time, it wasn't disorderly conduct, was it? It was for junk, wasn't it?

Gene: I guess—I mean, he's not really a junkie junkie. More of an addict. He never misses a gig.

Terry: He told me he doesn't have any gigs.

Gene: It's a little slow right now. No one works in September—the Jewish holidays.

Terry: Patsy says it's all over. Elvis. TV. L.A. Jazz is—

Gene: Patsy is just pissed off because she can't get Al or Bernie or Ziggy to quit so she had to go back to Stu who spends his day touching people's feet. Is that what you want me to do?

Terry: That's the same Bernie who got credit for your solos, isn't it?

Gene: Most likely. So *what*.

Terry: Why don't you send out those scripts you and Ziggy wrote?

Gene: They're not ready.

Terry: Do you want me to help?

Gene: Honey, you can barely speak English; no one understands a word you say. How the hell are you going to help with the scripts?

Terry: Fuck you.

Gene: What? Oh don't get upset. I'm just saying. Ziggy and I went to college. We know what we're doing. As soon as those scripts are ready—they're going out.

Terry: Do you have a gig for tonight?

Gene: Not yet.

Terry and Gene: Huh.

Gene: It happens. What's the big deal.

Terry: It's Saturday night.

Gene: The Jewish holidays. No one's working.

Terry: But it's Saturday night.

Gene: Terry, I've got my twenty weeks in, I subbed at the Copa twice last week, what's so goddamn important about Saturday night. Jesus—a gig is a gig.

Terry: You said if you ever weren't booked for a Saturday night, you'd quit the business.

Gene: Oh, come on. I never said that.

(She stares at him in disbelief, then anger)

Terry: You lying motherfucker—

Gene: Terry—

(She walks away from him)

Terry: You lying motherfucker—

(Terry doesn't see Gene as he moves toward her)

Gene: Terry, get a hold of your—

(He is suddenly next to her. She bats him away)

Terry: Get your hands off me, Dominic—

Gene: I'm Gene.

Terry: I don't care who you are. All of you. Stay away. I can't take this bullshit. All of you lie. All of you fucking lie.

Gene: STOP IT. Stop it.

(She snaps back to reality. Calms a bit)

Terry: What time is it?

Gene: Nine.

Terry: You have until midnight. If that phone doesn't ring, and you stay in the business, I'll fuckin' kill you. And I'll kill the baby. *(She takes her drink, and walks past Gene to the bedroom as Clifford sits)* I swear to God, I'll kill you both. *(She slams the bedroom door behind her.)*

End of ACT I

ACT TWO

ACT II

Same apartment, ten years later, with ten more years of inherited furniture, broken lamps, tchotchkes. Every surface is piled high; every inch of space below the couch or tables is crammed full as well.

Laid out on the couch—a very pale, dead Gene. Dressed in a tuxedo. Arms folded over his chest. The apartment is still. Dark.

Clifford: She didn't kill him that night, and she didn't kill me. Three months later, the doctor slapped me and I was on the scene. Gene was playing Sinatra at the Copa. She was finally going to get to hear Frankie, live. But on the night she was supposed to go, she started to get contractions. Around the time Sinatra and my dad were playing *Someone to Watch Over Me*, I was born. My dad never played Sinatra again, and to this day she's never seen him live. IT'S ALL MY FAULT. She was going to name me Francis Albert, but she was so pissed at me, she let Gene name me Clifford. After Clifford Brown. Now, Clifford Brown was a beautiful trumpet player, but Clifford has never been an easy name around the schoolyard. It might be OK for a forty-year-old shoe salesman, (*in the voice and/*

or manner of a child now) but on a ten-year-old seventh grader, which is what I am by now, 'cause I skipped two grades and everyone thinks I'm a genius who's gonna save the family, it's kind of lame.

(He crosses over to Gene who doesn't stir)

(NOTE: In the next several scenes, when Clifford interacts with his family, he does so as a child; when he talks to the audience, he finds a middle ground between the manner of a child and the ironic detachment of the adult Clifford.)

Clifford *(to audience)*: I liked bringing the guys from P.S. 145 to my apartment for their first time. I walk in with them, the house is dark—the house is always dark—and my father's lying like this. *(He points to the corpse-like Gene)* Freaked 'em out every time. *(To Gene)* Dad, wake up! Club date. You told me to wake you at six.

Terry *(loud)*: CLIFFORD! Clifford. My TV's fucked-up again. And check the oven.

Clifford: In a minute Ma. Dad, wake up! *(Looks at his father who doesn't budge)* He can sleep through anything. But in this house, that's a good way to go.

(Terry walks through now, in a robe. She is much older than she was. She's gained weight, and the last ten years have put a lot of mileage on her. She hands Clifford a glass)

Terry: Here, your poor old mother wants a refill.

(Clifford reluctantly takes the glass. Goes off-stage to the kitchen)

Terry: He fell asleep, timing your labor pains, did I ever tell you that?

Clifford *(from kitchen)*: A couple of thousand times, Ma.

Terry: Don't be such a smart-ass. You know, it's because of you, I never got to see Sinatra.

Clifford: Really? *(Hands her the drink)* I didn't know that. *(She walks to her off-stage bedroom)* Dad, come on—time to eat.

(Shakes his father a little. Gene comes to. He's older, but not nearly as worn as Terry)

Gene: Where am I?

Clifford: 1967. Saturday night. Club date. *(Whispers)* Lester Lanin.

Gene: Jesus, it's late. You should have woken me sooner. Lester hates it when I'm late.

Clifford: And you hate being there at all. So it works out.

(Clifford takes an oval tabletop from behind the couch and places it over the coffee table. Sets the table for dinner, then runs to the kitchen)

Gene: I do. I do hate him—did I tell you what Bernie does now? When Lester conducts, he doesn't conduct. You know, it bears no relation to the music, or any music, ever. Nobody in the band actually follows him. And he spends the whole night smiling and gladhanding his loyal, tone deaf fans—those people couldn't swing if you hung them.

Clifford (*off-stage*): Yeah, Dad, I know. But you're running late.

Terry (*off-stage*): Clifford!

Clifford (*off-stage*): Ma, it's almost done.

Gene: So two months ago, Lester's facing the dance floor, Bernie signals, and the entire horn section skips a beat. One and Two and One THREE FOUR. Like that. Lester turns around. *He knows something's wrong*, but since we did it in unison, he can't figure out what happened. We did it six more times, just to see if he'd catch on.

Clifford (*returning*): That's great Dad. You've got like, ten minutes for dinner. Here's your salad.

Terry (*off-stage*): Gene, don't forget to pick up cigarettes, and some "medicine" on your way home.

(*Clifford hands Gene a pencil and an index card from Gene's trumpet case*)

Gene: I wrote it down.

(Gene writes it down)

Clifford *(to audience)*: He has to write everything down, even "Take a shower", or he'll forget. When my mom really wants to get back at him, she hides his cards, and he has no idea what to do, or where to be, or who he is.

(Clifford runs to the kitchen. Gene finishes writing his note, now checks his wallet)

Terry *(off-stage)*: Get a fifth!

Gene: I only have eight bucks, I'll pick up a pint.

(Gene picks up his horn again. Before he can blow a note, she screams at him from the bedroom. It is a well-worn ritual)

Terry *(off-stage)*: Tomorrow's Sunday Gene. DON'T DO THIS TO ME. The stores are closed tomorrow.

Gene: You ought to be able to get by on a pint.

Terry *(off-stage)*: DON'T DO THIS TO ME, GENE. I WAS ON DOUBLE SHIFTS ALL FUCKING WEEK. I want to goddamn relax on my day off.

(Clifford returns with more plates, salad)

Gene *(looks at Clifford, whispers)*: Just 'til Monday. When I can get to the bank.

(Clifford nods. Reaches into his pocket. Gives his dad a five)

Terry *(off-stage)*: And don't take it from the kid.

Gene: It's taken care of Terry.

(Terry comes out of the bedroom, crosses to the kitchen)

Terry: Did you say you're working Lester Lanin?

Gene: Terry, would you let me practice. I'm late.

(He picks up the horn, starts to finger the valves)

Terry *(from the kitchen)*: You swore you wouldn't work for him again.

Gene: I told you I'm not working with him, it's just a club date. I don't even know who the leader is. *(Winks at Clifford)* Can I blow a couple of notes?

Terry *(from the kitchen)*: You shouldn't be practicing at six o'clock. THE NEWS IS ON.

Clifford: Ma. Do you need any help?

Terry *(from the kitchen)*: It's too fucking late to practice.

Clifford: Ma—we still have time to eat.

Terry *(from the kitchen)*: No. Your father has to practice. He couldn't practice earlier. Has to wait until my programs are on.

Gene: Terry, I just want to blow a few notes.

(Now she comes out from the kitchen, with hunks of lasagne on plates)

Terry: DON'T START IN WITH ME—ALL OF YOU. ALL OF YOU ARE IN THIS AGAINST ME.

("ALL OF YOU" refers to Clifford, and Gene, who are seated at the oval-topped coffee table. Which gives them little room to move. Terry—on fire—stands over the table. In one of her moods. Plates in hand)

Terry: Oh sure—no one notices what your father does to me. But when I get upset—you all think Terry has gone crazy. He's gas-lighting me.

Clifford: Ma, watch out!

(Terry tries to serve the food and yell at the same time. She loses her balance, falls, and knocks over the round fold-out table. Gene, in his tuxedo, instantly stands before anything stains him)

Terry: Sure. Now you move. You motherfucker. Nothing gets you. Nothing gets you.

(She runs through the living room to her bedroom. Slams the door. The whole apartment shakes. Father and son look at each other. Clifford gathers up what food he can. Bedroom door opens)

Terry: Enjoy your dinner—MOTHERFUCKERS!

*(She **slams** the door. Gene shakes his head. Sits down. Continues to eat his salad. He and Clifford converse, uninterrupted by her blasts)*

Clifford: Dad, how come you didn't practice before your nap?

(Gene, spaced out, blows on his salad fork. Door opens)

Terry *(yelling from bedroom)*: ASK YOUR FATHER!

(Slam)

Gene: I went to move the car. It took a while to find a space—so when I came home—

(Door opens)

Terry *(she's hysterical now)*: Enjoy your macaroni, MOTHERFUCKERS.

(Slam)

Clifford: What time did you leave to move the car?

Gene: I don't know—four, four-thirty.

Clifford *(exasperated)*: Dad, why do you do that? You know you can never find a space after four. It happens every time.

Gene: I got hung up with some—

Clifford: Yeah but Dad—you know she can't stand to hear you practice. She was out all day, working, you could have—

(Door opens)

Terry: THAT'S RIGHT, MOTHERFUCKER.

(Slam. The two of them sit there for a while. Eating slowly)

Terry *(off-stage)*: DOES ANYBODY LISTEN TO ME IN THIS FUCKING FAMILY?

Gene: Do we have a choice?

(The door opens. She's got an empty cup in her hand)

Terry: You better move your ass.

(She hurls the cup toward Gene—he ducks. It SMASHES against the wall)

Clifford *(to Gene)*: She broke bake-a-lite. *Nice Ma*, I didn't think that was possible.

(Gene tries to quiet Clifford)

Terry: DON'T GET CUTE WITH ME.

Gene: He wasn't getting cute with—

*(She grabs his trumpet case, shakes it, **and the horn goes crashing to the floor**)*

Clifford: Ma!

(Terry slams the door behind her. Gene rushes to his horn as if it were his child. Checks it carefully. It's OK. Now tuxedo neat, trumpet case in hand)

Gene: OK kiddo . . . thanks for cleaning up. I'd better get going. Try and get her to eat something.

Clifford *(nonchalant)*: OK. See you later.

(Gene leaves. Clifford picks up)

Clifford *(to audience)*: It's good for a family to have rituals. This was ours. Once, twice, three times a month. He'd screw up. She'd flip out. He'd leave for work. I'd clean up. She'd hide in the room. I'd bring her something to eat. She'd have a few drinks. Fall asleep. He'd sneak in around four A.M. Every once in a while she'd put furniture in front of the door. I'd wait until she'd fall asleep, and I'd move it so he could get in. If you got through the night without the cops coming, things were usually fine in the morning.

Terry *(from the bedroom)*: WHO are you talking to?

Clifford: It's just me, Ma.

(Lights up now on the basement of the Metropolitan Club, where Ziggy and Al arrive in matching powder blue tux jackets)

Al: Man, I had a bitch of a time parking.

Ziggy: Not me. I circled the island three timesh, drove over to Newark, and took a shubway in.

Gene *(arriving late)*: Hey, it's old home week.

Ziggy: The turtle hash landed.

Al: Hey, Gene Glimmer . . . *(Looks at his watch)* You're almost on time.

Ziggy: I didn't know you were doing thish gig.

Gene: Don't tell my wife. She thinks I'm a professional.

Ziggy: How'sh she and the kid doing? Haven't sheen Terry shince . . . the misshile crishish.

Gene: The family? The family's great.

(From upstairs, really bad 1967 rock music blares. They look up)

Al: Man, how'd three guys like us end up on a gig like this?

Ziggy: I think I'm retired and they forgot to tell me.

Gene: I tell people I'm in the twilight of a mediocre career.

(Gene takes out his horn. Starts to warm it up)

Al: The *bad* news is that rock band upstairs is going to close out the night. So, no overtime for us.

Gene: Good thing we're all rich.

Al: The *bad* news is that the parents want us to play three sets straight for the old farts.

Gene: Do they give us dinner?

Ziggy: Theshe people? They won't even let ush pee.

Gene: He's kidding, right?

Al: Rules of the club. Musicians can't use the facilities that the guests are using. And the kitchen toilet is busted, but the busboys have worked out a deal with the coffee shop across the street. So—

Ziggy: If we were black, they couldn't get away with thish.

Gene: It's not as bad as the Copa, at least they're not charging us for water.

Ziggy: The Copa: remember when Podel caught ush playing poker, and he ripped the card table out of the wall. Motherfucker couldn't shtand to shee a mushician have a good time.

Al: Those were the days. We closed that together, didn't we?

Gene: Are you kidding? Between us, I bet we closed every hotel, club, and ballroom in New York in the last 20 years.

(They think about this for a second)

(Lights down on the guys and up on the apartment. Clifford carries a dinner plate. Goes to the bedroom door)

Clifford: Mom, I got dinner.

(He puts the tray down. Slowly forces the door open. It's pitch black. Terry's not in her bed. He looks up and sees her now. She is sitting on the windowsill. Her legs are off the ground. The window is wide open, and nine stories up)

Terry: That's right. I know what I'm doing. He'll finally be sorry for what he's done to me.

(Clifford sticks his head out the adjacent window to talk to her)

Clifford: Ma.

(She gets upset)

Terry: Clifford, get your head back inside.

(He does)

Clifford: Mom—that's not a good place to sit.

Terry: I won't be sitting here long.

Clifford: I brought you dinner.

Terry: He's not supposed to practice after six o'clock. Even the social worker told him that.

Clifford: I know—

Terry (*suddenly maternal, worried*): Is the oven off? You have to be very careful with that oven. It's not safe. That's how my eyebrows got burned.

Clifford: I know Ma—I remember—

Terry: Fucking landlord. Your father wouldn't sue. We could have made a fucking fortune. But no— not your—

Clifford: He felt really bad about screwing up tonight.

Terry: Bullshit he did. You stay away from me. Don't try to con me out of this. I've been dead for fifteen years.

(*She starts to cry. Throws a tissue on the floor. He inches to the windowsill*)

Clifford: You saving these tissues for anything? Or can I throw them out?

Terry: Is that supposed to be funny?

Clifford: The ziti came out pretty good. But I think you may have over-cooked the noodles—maybe it's a little . . .

Terry: *Mushad?*

Clifford: Maybe a little. What do you think? Why don't you come in from there and taste it?

Terry: He hasn't taken me out to dinner in fifteen years.

Clifford: Ma—you're too good a cook. Just taste it.

Terry: Oh, Clifford.

Clifford: Ma, please . . .

(She turns to him and lets him gently pull her in from the sill)

Terry: You shouldn't have to do this.

Clifford: It's OK, Ma.

Terry: He should do this. Not you.

(She starts to cry. He holds her)

Clifford: He's at work. It's OK, Ma. It's OK.

(Back over to the Metropolitan Club where Ziggy, Al, and Gene have finished their sets. They're exhausted)

Ziggy: Al, you all right?

Al: He's a sadist.

(Al is particularly beat)

Gene: Fucking Lester does everything at the same tempo, how can he not know that trumpets need a rest once in a while?

Ziggy: Theshe motherfuckersh know, they jusht don't give a shit. You heard what happened with the circush? They come into Madishon Shquare Garden lasht month—add an extra show a day; and you know that booksh a killer: Shcreaming F'sh and G'sh all night. No breaksh. Firsht week, two trumpet playersh passh out, one hash a shtroke. The other getsh Bellsh Palshy.

Gene: What did the union do?

(Ziggy looks at Gene, incredulous)

Ziggy: Thoshe motherfuckersh? They're all getting greashed.

Gene: Yeah, but still. We pay dues.

(Ziggy looks at him: Gene's hopeless. He tries Al)

Ziggy: Finally, after a *third* kid bushts a vein in hish head, the NLRB people come in, and shay either the circush doublesh the hornsh, and shplitsh the book, or they have to shupply the trumpet shection with presshurized shuitsh.

Gene: Well, I gotta get going. I promised the family I'd be home early.

(Gene stands, they shake hands)

Al: Hey, tell Terry I'm expecting a tray of lasagne for Christmas.

Ziggy: And tell her I may want my lampsh back.

Gene: If you can find them . . . you can keep 'em.

(Gene starts to leave)

Al: Wait a minute, I forgot to tell you: Jonesy's back in town. He's playing piano over at the Melody Lounge.

Gene: Jonesy? His chops were just never the same after . . .

Ziggy: After they bushted hish chopsh.

Al: But dig this. He gave me this tape, it's going around. Brownie. Clifford. Some guys in Philly found this live recording of him, from the night he died.

Gene: Not the *Night in Tunisia* solo?

(Al pulls out a small, old-fashioned cassette player)

Al: Just listen, you're not gonna believe this.

(Al hits the play button on Clifford Brown's last recording of A Night in Tunisia. *After a few notes)*

Ziggy: That'sh Clifford!

(Now, chorus after inventive chorus. It is one thing to listen to this unbelievable recording. It is another thing entirely to watch three life-long jazz trumpet players listen to this fabled lost masterpiece for the first time. Every turn Brownie takes causes them to shake their heads, laugh, murmur. They listen and react to every nuance of this solo with an intensity and passion that is otherwise not part of their lives)

Ziggy: Can you believe—

Al: Wait wait wait.

(They are astonished by his level of musicianship. It brings tears to their eyes. The swiftness of their reactions, and the depth of their understanding of what Brownie is playing, tells us something about these three musicians as well. For all their joking and fucking up, they have a profound connection to their music, one they can only share with each other. Every time Ziggy and Gene think Clifford Brown has reached a musical climax, Al says . . .)

Al: Wait wait wait.

(Brownie plays through the turn around. Plays another chorus . . . Gene in particular laughs at every quote

*within the solo. He smiles at the way Clifford threads
his long melodic lines through the chords. Ziggy nudges
Al to watch how Gene takes in the nuances. Each phrase
builds on the one before it. Brownie takes another chorus,
and the musicians are staggered)*

Al: Motherfucker. That is one motherfucker.

(Gene is in ecstasy. Finally, Clifford all but ignites)

Ziggy: That's it. I quit.

*(Freeze. Back at the apartment: Clifford tiptoes out of the
bedroom. He goes to the TV, turns it on, lowers the
volume down to zero. Then he goes to the couch, wraps
himself in a blanket, and sits staring at the TV until
Gene comes home)*

Gene: Hey kiddo. You're still up? I had the worst
time finding a parking place. I must have clocked
three miles just looking for a space. But I finally
found one that's good 'til Tuesday.

Clifford: That's good Dad.

Gene: Tough gig. Lester has no idea how to pace
a band. Hey—the place looks good. Thanks for
cleaning up.

Clifford: Sure.

Gene: How's she doing?

Clifford: Fine.

Gene: Is it OK for me to go in there?

Clifford: She finally fell asleep.

Gene: Do you think it's all right then?

Clifford: I guess.

Gene: Heard the wildest cassette tonight. Al brought it in. Clifford Brown—your namesake. I'd always heard that the night he died, you know he died in a car crash—

Clifford: I know. With Richie Powell. Ten years ago.

Gene: He was only twenty-five. And he was clean. Has it been that long?

Clifford: It was right before I was born, that's why you named me—

Gene: You're not ten. Are you ten already?

Clifford: Dad . . .

Gene: Wow.

(Gene disappears into space for a moment. Clifford waits)

Gene: Ten years. Hmmn. They said the night he died, he played as if he knew he was going to die. That he must've known, because anyone who was there, it was in the back of a music store in Philly, people who were there said it was . . . they never heard anything like it in their lives. People have talked about that solo like it's one of the lost wonders of jazz. Well—it turns out some guy recorded it on wire, and Al got a tape of it. You're not going to believe this . . .

(Goes to the cassette player. Puts it in)

Gene: His last night on earth. Dig this—

(A Night in Tunisia comes on. Clifford listens with his father. They shake their heads in awe at what they hear. Clifford laughs at the same spots Al and Ziggy did. He has inherited his father's understanding of the music. They get so caught up in the playing, that neither notice Terry as she emerges from her dark room. She punches the music off. Gene and Clifford look up, terrified)

Terry: Where the fuck have you been?

Gene: It went overtime. You know these things.

Terry: You went out with the guys. Had fun. I'm home alone and you went out with the guys. Was Patsy there?

Gene: Terry, please—

Terry: She always had a thing for you.

Gene: Terry, Patsy had a thing for everyone.

Terry: Don't get smart with me. Did you bring me my bottle?

(She starts for his trumpet case. Gene grabs it before she can get to it. He opens the trumpet case. Hands her a bottle)

Terry: What is this?

Gene: Sherry—it's what they had—

Terry: I don't drink sherry—

Gene: You don't drink that?

Terry: Not for two years.

Gene: What difference does it make, booze is booze Terry.

Terry: What the fuck is that supposed to mean?

Gene *(to Clifford)*: Poison is poison.

Terry: And you're so fucking clean, Gene. A monk. Gene's so sweet. Gene is so clean. Bullshit. Fifteen years of your bullshit and lies: "It's just slow right now. Wait until this record comes out. Every TV station will have a band.

We'll go on vacation next year. You shouldn't be
tired, you're a waitress, not a doctor. We'll get our
own furniture." YOU AND YOUR FUCKING LIES.
(*To Clifford*) Your father hasn't touched me in ten
years. I'VE HAD IT. DO YOU HEAR ME. ALL OF
YOU.

(*She takes the sherry, and pours it over the living room.
She soaks the rug. She starts to light her cigarette. (She
looks at the match. Then at the rug. She throws the
match on the rug)*)

Clifford: Ma!

Terry: Francis, you stay out of this.

(*She lights another, and another. Flings them at the rug,
at Gene; she fails to start a fire and finally throws the
whole box of matches to the floor*)

Terry: Get away from me. Get away from me. Goddamn it. You got the wrong booze. If you'd gotten
bourbon this whole fucking place would be on fire
by now.

(*Terry breaks down in a wail of tears. Clifford steps
downstage; he is no longer a child. Over Clifford's
monologue, we hear Gene playing* Willow Weep for
Me)

Clifford (*now an adult again, to audience*): I had to
call an ambulance that night. They came and took
Mom away. She talked herself out in a couple of
weeks. After a while, she started to call them her-

self, when she was losing it. If they didn't come fast enough, she'd call again and tell them—

Terry: 10–13, 10–13! Officer Down! *OFFICER DOWN! (To Clifford)* That'll bring'em in a hurry.

Clifford *(to audience)*: It went on like this, for years. Through high school, through college. And I never got away.

(Terry and Gene circle each other warily in the living room, then exit)

Clifford: I kept hoping they'd be like old Generals at war, finally realizing they're all they have; that their memories of how they tried and failed to kill each other would eventually give them a bond. It didn't work that way. Even after college, when I finally moved out, the farthest I could get was across the street. I was still on duty. *(A phone rings. Clifford crosses to phone)* The four A.M. phone call. The second the phone rings, you know you're in for a long night. And you've been trained since birth to handle it. *(Into phone)* "Yes officer. You've found my mother naked on Amsterdam Avenue? Uh-huh. She wants you to put her on a bus so she can join a convent in Montana? OK. Well, don't do that. What emergency room is she in? Fine. I'll be right up. Thank you."

(Clifford hangs up the phone and crosses to his mother in an emergency room. She's completely wrecked)

Clifford: You OK?

Terry: What the fuck are you doing here?

Clifford: I don't know.

Terry: I never should have married your father—

Clifford: It's a little late Ma.

Terry: Motherfucker booked a club date on our anniversary. How could he *forget* our anniversary?

Clifford *(to audience)*: She has a point.

Terry: WHO ARE YOU TALKING TO?

Clifford: Sorry, Ma.

Terry: I have had it with all of you motherfuckers. I want to go to a convent. In Minnesota—

Clifford: I thought it was Montana.

Terry: It's one of those "M" states in the middle there, Clifford. Don't give me a hard time. I told the bastards to just put me on a bus. But they *had* to call you.

Clifford: It's OK. I was up anyway.

(She starts to cry)

Terry: I'm sorry. Clifford. I've lost it again, haven't I? (*Clifford doesn't answer*) It's his fault.

Clifford: He tries Ma.

Terry: You know the worst part, once you've been in a nuthouse? Every time something feels wrong, you don't know—is it wrong, or are you going crazy again . . . you just don't know.

(*She starts to sob. Stands over Clifford now*)

Terry: Make sure I get a roomate who smokes, Clifford.

Clifford: I'll see what I can do.

Terry: I used to tell your father, it wasn't right, that you had to do this. You know what your father said: "That's why you have kids Terry, so they'll take care of you." You never should have saved me Clifford. I've been dead for thirty years anyway.

(*Terry exits*)

Clifford (*to audience*)**:** I went to work; I was two hours late. No one noticed. I spent the morning writing ads. At lunchtime, I went in to a stairwell and cried. For the first time in twenty years. I finished the afternoon, like nothing happened.

(*Clifford, now with Gene, who's more spaced-out than usual*)

Clifford: Couldn't you tell that she was losing it, before she—

Gene: How can you tell? It's irrational.

Clifford: You ran out of insurance. They want to send her upstate.

Gene: She'll talk her way out of it.

Clifford: They won't let her come home if you're here.

Gene: You know, she drinks.

Clifford: *Really?*

Gene: After she flipped out, I found bottles all over the place.

Clifford: What?

Gene: Things just got—the boozing, the flip outs—I just thank God it started after you left home.

Clifford: Are you *serious?*

Gene: It didn't get bad 'til the last couple of years.

Clifford: Dad, you're nuts. That's just not . . . she's had a drinking problem since I can remember.

Gene: Clifford, I think I would know that.

Clifford: I DON'T.

Gene *(changing the subject)*: So what do you want to do?

Clifford: What do *you* want to do? She's your wife.

Gene: She won't talk to me when she's like this. She's completely irrational. You know that.

Clifford: Why does it have to be up to me?

Gene: You're the son. She's your mother. Who else is there?

Clifford: Dad, what the fuck is your problem, she's your wife. SHE'S YOUR WIFE and if we don't do something, she's gone. Do you get it? DO YOU UN-DERSTAND WHAT'S GOING ON?

(Gene spaces out)

Clifford: Are you listening to me?

Gene: There's no reason to get upset. You always figure something out. You're the RED CROSS.

(Gene stares into space. There is a long, awkward pause)

Clifford: OK, get your horn, you're out.

Gene: I'm sorry?

Clifford: Get your fuckin' horn, and get out.

Gene: What are you talking about?

Clifford: Dad, she can't live with you. She can't get a place on her own. I'm not letting them send her upstate. You're out. It's over.

Gene: Clifford.

Clifford: It's over. As of tonight. Call Ziggy. Call Al. I don't give a fuck. Call someone. You're out of here. (*He packs the horn, gives it to Gene*) Dad, she's coming, you're going. You two are done.

Gene: I don't think it's that bad.

Clifford: You don't think, Dad. You don't know. YOU DON'T HAVE A FUCKING CLUE. (*He pushes the case into Gene and knocks Gene backward*) You don't have a fucking clue.

(*Gene stares at Clifford, completely in shock. Gene walks out. Clifford steps forward*)

Clifford (*to audience*): Before that night, I had never yelled at my father. And yelling at him . . . if my mom couldn't get through to him in thirty years, I wasn't going to either. That night, at midnight, I drove him over to Ziggy's. I don't think he had any idea what was going on. It was like moving a cat. In two weeks, Terry got out. I took her home, stayed with her the first couple of nights. After I left, she went right back to drinking. Meanwhile, Ziggy told me he and Gene were going at it pretty good down in Hell's Kitchen.

(Gene and Ziggy enter, face off)

Ziggy: Did you get bananash?

Gene: No, I got hung up at the bank . . . there was a line. Then by the time I went to move the car . . .

Ziggy: *Why* do you go the bank at three P.M. on a Friday?

Gene: I always go to the bank on Friday.

Ziggy: Fridaysh' pay day, Genie. For shtraight people. It'sh a mob shcene.

Gene: Is that true? I always wondered why it was crowded, but—everyone gets paid on Friday?

Ziggy: That'sh it—

Gene *(sees Ziggy leaving)*: Where are you going?

Ziggy: It's rush hour, I'm going to go get a few sheats on the shubway! *(To Clifford)* I don't know how your old lady put up with him.

(Ziggy and Gene exit)

Clifford *(to audience)*: She didn't. But she couldn't make it without him either. She kept drinking for a few more years, finally fell into a coma. Liver shut off. Lung cancer. The works. Naturally, she came out of it. Quit drinking, denies ever having had a drinking problem. And still smokes three packs a

day. She still makes a decent lasagne. And Genie
...I haven't seen him in five years... (*He looks to
the off-stage bandstand.* I Remember Clifford *plays.
We're back to 1985 at the bar of the Melody Lounge*) He
looks the same, and...he still plays a pretty
horn...

(*Patsy re-joins him*)

Patsy: He's playing *I Remember Clifford.*

Clifford: Genie on a ballad, break your heart every
time.

Patsy: How are you? Are you happy?

Clifford (*never been asked this before*)**:** What?

Patsy: Are you happy?

Clifford: I'm always fine.

(*They listen to Gene's solo*)

Patsy: He plays it every time.

Clifford (*amazed*)**:** He does?

(*Clifford and Patsy listen as Gene finishes the last few
notes of* I Remember Clifford. *When he finishes playing, they applaud. She takes him across the stage to the
booth*)

Gene (*off-stage*)**:** Thank you folks. That was *I Remember Clifford.* We'd like to welcome you to the

Melody Lounge. We're going to take a short break so you all can catch your breath, and we'll be right back.

(Clifford and Patsy applaud again as Ziggy, and Gene trailing behind, crosses over to the bar. Gene walks right past his son, does not see him)

Clifford *(standing)*: Dad.

Ziggy: Turtle, your shon ish here.

Clifford: Yo, Dad—

(Gene stares for a second, at last sees his son—six feet away)

Gene: Hey . . . Clifford.

Clifford: Yeah. I . . . I was going to call you, before I—to let you know, but . . . You sounded good.

Gene: Not any more.

(Ziggy tries to sneak by them to Patsy in the booth. Gene collars him)

Gene: Hey, Ziggy, Al brought in a tape last week—air-check from Thornhill's band—I guess I used to blow, back then.

Ziggy *(on the way to Patsy's booth)*: Oh bullshit—you shtill shound good. *(To Clifford)* He'sh shtill driving me crazy.

(Ziggy goes to the booth. Gene and Clifford have another awkward moment, alone together)

Clifford: How come Al's on drums?

Gene: He had a mini-stroke, so . . .

Clifford: I'm sorry—

Gene: There's many fewer high notes on the drums . . . Did you see Patsy? *(Turns to the booth)* Hey, Patsy, the *k-i-d* is here.

(Gene leads Clifford over to the booth as Al and Jonesy join Patsy and Ziggy there. The gang is all there, but much the worse for wear)

Patsy: I know—old home week.

Al *(showing the effects of his stroke)*: Gene—I told Patsy we'd let her sing with the band once the place is completely empty.

Ziggy: Do you all remember Genie'sh boy?

Jonesy: Is that Frankie? Jesus Christ. I knew you when your dick was this big.

(He holds up one third of his pinky. Everyone laughs)

Ziggy: Hish name ish Clifford, after Clifford Brown.

Jonesy: It was supposed to be Francis Albert, but then the night you were born—

Clifford: I know the story.

Jonesy: I'll bet you do—hey, how's Terry doing?

Clifford: (*deflecting, to Patsy*) How's Stu?

Patsy: He died on me a year ago.

Clifford: That's a bitch. I'm sorry to hear it.

Patsy: He was going to start playing again, after he retired.

Al: You guys heard Bernie is in the hospital? In Germany. Cancer.

Jonesy: No. I didn't know that.

Al: Yeah, he's been living over there for years. Some teaching gig.

Jonesy: Who else died? (*To Clifford*) It's our favorite game.

Ziggy (*trying to give Gene and Clifford some privacy*): Uh fellash, let'sh a—the shooner we go back in, the—

Patsy: What should I sing?

Clifford: My mom had a request.

Al and Ziggy: *Just My Fucking Luck?*

Clifford: Nope.

Jonesy and Patsy: *Why Was I Born?*

Clifford: Bingo.

Ziggy: Fellash—Patshy—two tunesh in, you're on.

(The guys head up onto the bandstand. Gene, the slowest, lags behind. Clifford stops him)

Clifford: Dad . . . *(They look at each other)* It's been a while.

Gene: You're busy. Work. Your job's—

Clifford: I quit.

Gene: You quit? Are you gonna be able to collect—

Clifford: I'm gonna go west—work on the . . . painting stuff. I was hoping you'd look in on her once in a while.

(Gene thinks about this)

Gene: You were good with those collages you know.

(Clifford can't believe his father noticed)

Clifford: Huh?

Gene: Not just me—your mother always thought that's what you were gonna do.

Clifford: It's just cut and paste . . . see how it goes. How've you—

Gene: You'll be fine—keep your nut small, pay your dues, as long as you have a place to paint . . .

(They look at each other)

Gene: How's she look?

Clifford: OK, so-so . . . she gave me some lasagne, to give you.

Gene *(thinks about Terry)*: Terry. She . . . *(Gene is suddenly overwhelmed. An instant later he seals it up.)* OK kiddo. Thanks for . . .

(They have an awkward choice: to hug good-bye or to shake hands. They stop. Start. Finally, Gene just turns and goes up toward the bandstand)

Clifford: Dad—*Why was I born?*

Gene: I'll play it. Two tunes in. Good to see you kiddo.

Clifford: If you think of it, call her in the morning, say thanks.

(Gene heads up onto the bandstand)

Clifford: He's not going to remember to call her. But I have to ask, same way I ask Mom to come and hear him play.

(Lights up on Terry in her bedroom doorway, smoking a cigarette, alone)

Terry: Leave your poor old lady alone Clifford. I'm not going over there to hear that rat-bastard play. Thirty years he never took me out. *(She stops)* And besides, if I hear him play—I get all . . . *(She starts to cry)* You go. Godspeed, caro figlio.

(She snuffs out her cigarette, as the lights go out on her)

Clifford: So long, Ma. *(To audience)* Like I said: no clean breaks.

(Clifford crosses to the bar, listens to Gene onstage as he starts to play It Never Entered My Mind. *We see a silhouette of Gene playing behind a scrim)*

Clifford: When he's up there, blowing, he's totally in touch with everything that's going on around him. Ziggy bends a note, he echos it instantly. A car horn sounds outside, he puts it into his solo, or harmonizes under it, a second later. I used to wonder how he could sense everything while he was blowing, and almost nothing when he wasn't. Now I just wonder how many more chances will I have to hear him blow. If I have kids . . .

These guys are not even an endangered species any more. It's too late. There are no more big bands, no more territory bands. No more nonets, or tentets. No more sixty weeks a year on the road. No more jam sessions 'til dawn in the Cincinnati Zoo. When they go, that'll be it.

No one will even understand what they were doing. A fifty year blip on the screen. Men who mastered their obsession, who ignored, or didn't even notice anything else. They played not for fame, and certainly not for money. They played for each other. To swing. To blow. Night after night, they were just burning brass. Oblivious.

(The lights come down on the Melody Lounge as the music comes up)

The End